CARAVAN

DINING ALL DAY

CHRIS AMMERMANN
To Laura, Arlo & Otis. Dad and Merle and my mother, Jennifer.

LAURA HARPER-HINTON
To Chris and my beautiful sons, Arlo & Otis. To Mum and Dad.

MILES KIRBY
For my loves Renée, Eli and Marlon, and for Ma and Pa Kirby.

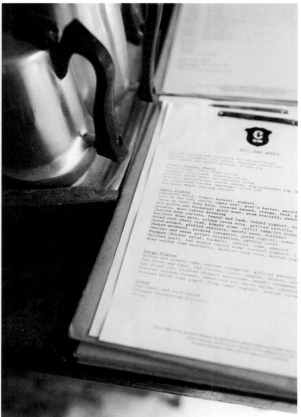

DINING ALL DAY

Our version of all-day dining has come from a number of places, and is the foundation of what we wanted to provide to our local neighbourhoods. At the heart of an all-day dining restaurant is the notion that a space must transition from morning into night while feeling comfortable and warm at all times of the day. Our first restaurant was designed with this in mind, but on an extremely tight budget; the three of us put every penny we had (which wasn't much) into the project. We started from a premise of using recycled, reclaimed and repurposed materials, the combination of which created a space that already felt like it had been there forever – it had warmth and honesty and was pared back in a soft, timeless way. We have taken these principles and aesthetics to our other restaurants and have created soft industrial interiors that feel comfortable and lived in, where a cup of coffee in the morning is just as plausible and enjoyable as a late-night cocktail.

Another source of inspiration for opening all-day dining restaurants was the long years we spent working in the restaurant industry; we finished at odd times, we took breaks at odd times and we often ate at odd times. We so often found ourselves on a precious break, only to be told that the kitchen was closed. At Caravan, the kitchen is never closed and you can dine with us whenever it suits you. It is an intentional 'do as you please' approach that is fluid, flexible and welcoming.

By encouraging dining throughout the day, you also attract a wonderful mix of people and a continuous energy in the room. During the course of a day our spaces are filled with coffee drinkers, paper readers, professionals in for breakfast meetings and business lunches, parents with buggies, laptop workers, creatives and students, evening diners and cocktail swillers. Some are with us for half an hour, others stay quite literally all day! All are welcome, any time.

A NOTE ON SHARING AND SMALL PLATES

We all have young kids, which makes for a rather busy existence when trying to run restaurants and a coffee roastery at the same time. However, like many people with busy lives, we just crack on; we work hard, play hard (when time allows) and spend as much family time as we can. Something that struck us when we were writing this introduction was the notion of sharing. It's a concept that as adults we are constantly (often unsuccessfully) trying to in-grain in our young children. Obviously it's a solid principle, and persevere we shall, but it's also quite odd that we are so obsessed with imparting this to our children. As adults, we are not very good at sharing and don't always set the best example. Food and sharing food together, however, is a unifier and breaks that all down. In fact, we often bend over backwards to let someone else eat the last croquette or devour the final delicious morsel of scallop ceviche.

We designed the mainly small plate sharing menu at Caravan with precisely this in mind. People love to share food together, so why restrict them to their own individual starter, main course and pudding if they would prefer to share? Of course because we truly want people to dine however and whenever they want, we added some large plates to the menu for good measure. But the majority of people who dine with us share all the dishes they order, large or small. We love that it creates such a convivial, warm atmosphere of mutual enjoyment and discussion about the food and ingredients being eaten. It is easy to see why so many cultures prefer to eat like this. And in our world of bite-sized pieces of information and our thirst for fast, easy satisfaction, who can deny the appeal of having lots of different flavour combinations in one social, gratifying dining sess-ion? We encourage you to use the recipes in this book in a similar fashion. Create your own sharing lunch, brunch and dinner feasts, combining recipes that you feel will complement each other. Set your own globally inspired menu – there are no rules!

WELL TRAVELLED

One of the first questions you get asked when you tell someone that you own a restaurant, is 'what kind of food do you serve?' It's a logical question; restaurants are so much about the food, and people like to associate a restaurant with a particular cuisine style so they know what to expect when they walk through the door. It wasn't until at least a year into opening our first restaurant that we settled on a phrase that we felt perfectly encapsulated our food and drink concept. It's not that we had changed our food philosophy; in fact, this was exactly where the name Caravan – something you explore and discover with – had come from in the first place. It just took us a while to land on something that felt right and that

people understood straight away. So now when we get asked what kind of food we serve, we say 'well travelled'. When diners step through our restaurant doors, we like to think we take them on a culinary journey that weaves its way around the world, showcasing flavours and inspiration from our home country, New Zealand, and our own global travels. Our menus are full of fresh produce, bold flavours and magpie influence – we love the freedom that we get by not tying ourselves to any particular cuisine style or geographical region. The recipes in this cookbook are representative of our free cooking style and travel-inspired creations. They are truly what the Caravan picked up along the way.

ON COFFEE

Coffee is an obsession for us. One of our proudest moments was opening the doors at our Exmouth Market restaurant and serving our very first breakfasts, with coffee that we had lovingly roasted ourselves on site. A number of people at the time considered it an odd proposition a coffee roastery combined with a restaurant? But for us, it was a logical and complementary combining of two true passions – food and coffee. Coffee at restaurants and cafés can so often be a disappointment; we wanted to control the process from start to finish and provide an excellent coffee experience for all our customers.

Roasting the coffee on site, initially in the basement of our Exmouth Market location, then at the back of our converted grain store in King's Cross, was a natural decision for us. We wanted to engage with our customers about coffee and to display a sense of honesty, openness and exploration around the processing and production of coffee. By presenting coffee in an unpretentious, candid way, you can start a dialogue with people and hopefully develop and grow their understanding of what those in the specialty coffee world are offering.

Over the years our roasting business, Caravan Coffee Roasters, has grown with our restaurants and our wonderful team of talented coffee professionals. So too have our philosophies and objectives. Our aim, ultimately, was always to encourage as many people as possible to participate in the discussion about and enjoyment of specialty coffee. This is unchanged, and we encourage our baristas, coffee roasters, coffee trainers, waiters, chefs and managers to engage with our guests about specialty coffee, our passion for it and how a cup of well made, freshly roasted coffee is such a beautiful and fulfilling thing. Spreading the word in an engaging, enthusiastic way has always been our approach to recruiting more specialty coffee drinkers.

What we have honed over the years is how we, as coffee roasters, coffee graders, coffee sourcers and coffee importers, participate in the world of specialty coffee. For us the key thing is sourcing the best quality coffee we can in the most sustainable, social and ethical way. The vast majority of our coffee is now directly sourced. This means we have visited the farms where the coffee is grown, met with the farmers and engaged in a dialogue with them about quality and sustainability, and assured ourselves that the coffee is ethically grown, harvested and processed. We discuss with the farmers the challenges they face, improvements that can be made to production, harvesting, maintaining consistent quality and coffee prices, and how we can help in that process. Our passion for coffee extends well beyond the joy of a beautifully produced single-origin filter coffee, to the talented people that have participated in the creation of the bean along the way.

With this in mind, we take our role as coffee roasters (but not ourselves!) seriously. Our goal is to showcase the care, craft and hard work that has gone into producing a green bean ready for roasting, and to bring out the wonderful flavours and characteristics that are locked inside through the roasting process. Many forget that coffee is a fruit, and what we as roasters are always striving for is to bring out the unique flavours and nuances of that fruit and for our customers to really taste them in the cup.

For us, the craft of making and serving great coffee is as much a part of Caravan as anything else. People come to us for their daily takeout or to sit in, working or dining and enjoying unique filters and espresso coffees, throughout the day and night. It is a harmonious and complementary ingredient that makes Caravan what it is.

OUR PEOPLE

It sounds like a cliché, but for good reason. Anyone who owns a restaurant, or any business for that matter, will understand the importance that people – your people – have in the success of an operation.

In the seven years since we opened our first restaurant and coffee roastery we have been lucky enough to share our journey with some of the most committed and passionate chefs, waiters, managers, kitchen porters, coffee roasters, coffee trainers, coffee graders, baristas and bar tenders in the business. We now employ over 200 people and every one of those beautiful souls makes Caravan what it is. Without the energy, passion and dedication that these talented individuals bring, day and night, to the restaurants and coffee roastery, none of it happens.

To all of you, past and present, who have contributed via a recipe, a plating style, a drink, a system, a coffee profile, a joke or a shoulder to cry on in our brief history, we thank you wholeheartedly. You know who you are, please take a bow for your efforts, your talents and all the hard work.

MORNING BREW

The concept of an all-day restaurant that roasts its own coffee in-house has its roots in the long-established and thriving café and coffee scene of our home country, New Zealand. Good coffee is such an intrinsic part of our culture that it was easily one of things we missed the most when first arriving in the UK 16 years ago. We wanted to jump straight in and open a coffee roastery and restaurant, serving amazing coffee to the uninitiated. Looking back now, we are glad we waited and spent those defining and valuable years immersing ourselves in London hospitality. We ate and drank our way around town and travelled extensively throughout Europe and around the world before opening our first coffee roastery and restaurant in Exmouth Market in 2010. The specialty coffee scene was just starting to take off in London and, by combining our own in-house coffee roastery with our other passion, food and booze, we created some-thing previously unseen in London.

For us, coffee sits alongside our food and drink in equal measures and so it felt right for the first chapter of the book to be all about that very important ritual – The Morning Brew. We have included a home filter brew recipe, using one of our favourite easy-to-use pieces of equipment. By making a few simple adjustments to your morning coffee routine, you can vastly improve your coffee experience and (we think) your day.

The food recipes in this chapter are classics that have become staples on our takeout counters over the years and are definitely best when enjoyed with a cup of your favourite coffee.

1

Weigh 32g of coffee using the scales, grind it to a reasonably coarse grind size; this should have the consistency of rough sand. Place the filter paper into the Chemex. Pour freshly boiled water through the filter, this will get rid of the slight paper taste, and preheat the Chemex. Without removing filter, discard the water from the Chemex. Add the ground coffee into the Chemex.

2

The boiled water will have now cooled down to the ideal temperature of 91–94°C. Place the Chemex onto the scales, and tare (re-set the scale to zero). Start the timer and slowly begin to pour 50–70g of water onto the coffee grinds.

3

When pouring, ensure all grinds are saturated, whilst trying to avoid pouring down the sides of the filter paper. The coffee grinds will start to 'bloom' (increase in size); this is the trapped CO_2 gas created during the roasting process departing. Allow the bloom to sit, avoiding it drying out.

4

Before the bloom dries out (roughly 30–40sec), start pouring the rest of the heated water. Apply the remaining water in a circular motion, tracking between the inside edge and centre of the Chemex. It should take around 1 minute 40 seconds to reach the total amount of water needed (500g). Avoid moving the Chemex during the process; this will allow the water to pass through the bed of coffee without disruption.

5

When the bed of coffee is dry, remove the filter paper from the Chemex and discard.

6

Give the Chemex a quick swirl to aerate the coffee before serving, and pour.

COCONUT, FRUIT AND NUT GRANOLA BAR

There are so many delicious ingredients packed into these bars, which makes every bite a joy. They are a great snack to have on hand as they are prepared the day before and last well in the fridge for up to week. It is really important to check the texture of the bar before placing in the fridge to set. If the mixture is crumbly when it goes into the fridge, it will be crumbly when it comes out. Pressing the mixture firmly into the tray is important to ensure the right consistency.

MAKES 12–14
160g coconut oil
35g caster sugar
35g muscovado sugar
250g golden syrup
100g pitted Medjool dates,
chopped into thirds
125g jumbo oats
100g desiccated coconut
80g dried apricots, chopped
into quarters
40g dried cranberries
25g dried goji berries
80g raisins
30g walnuts, roughly chopped
30g pecans, roughly chopped
30g shelled pistachio nuts, whole

1 Oil and line a 20cm square baking tray with baking paper.

2 Put the coconut oil, sugars, golden syrup and dates in a pan and gently heat to dissolve the sugars. Remove from the heat and set aside.

3 Put all the remaining ingredients into a large bowl and mix well before adding the wet mixture. Mix until well combined. Test the consistency is right by tightly squeezing a handful of mixture to see if it binds. If it does not, add a little more golden syrup.

4 Press the mixture evenly and firmly into the baking tray and place in the fridge overnight to set. In the morning, turn the bar out onto a chopping board and use a sharp knife to portion as you see fit. This will keep in an airtight container in the fridge for up to a week.

SPELT, KALE, FETA AND PINE NUT MUFFIN

This muffin started life as a salad; we felt the combination of flavours was so good that a muffin must be made too; similar ingredients have made their way on to our pizzas as well. The result is a deliciously moist, tangy muffin, making it a great alternative to sweet muffins. As with all muffins, they are best enjoyed warm from the oven slathered in butter. If you don't have spelt flour to hand, you can use plain flour or wholemeal which also yields great results, in fact playing around with a couple of different flours can really add to the flavour of these muffins – feel free to get creative.

MAKES 12

180g curly kale
230g plain flour
200g white spelt flour
2 tsp baking powder
5g fine sea salt
3 eggs
300ml whole milk
330g Greek yoghurt
250ml vegetable oil
150g Cheddar, grated
150g feta cheese, crumbled
50g pine nuts, toasted

1   Preheat the oven to 180°C and butter a 12-hole muffin tray or individual muffin tins.

2   Blanch the curly kale in a large pan of boiling salted water for 2 minutes. Drain and refresh in cold water, then drain again, squeezing out as much excess moisture from the kale as you can. Roughly chop and set aside.

3   Sift the flours and baking powder into a medium bowl. Add the salt and stir together so everything is evenly mixed.

4   Lightly whisk the eggs in a large mixing bowl, then whisk in the milk, yoghurt and oil.

5   Mix the flours into the wet ingredients and stir well until all the flour is mixed into the wet. Fold the Cheddar, feta, kale and half the pine nuts into the mixture.

6   Divide the mixture evenly between the 12 muffin tins and then scatter over the remaining pine nuts. Immediately place in the oven and bake for 20–25 minutes. Check to see if they are ready by inserting a wooden skewer into the centre of a muffin; if the skewer comes out clean, they are ready.

7   Remove from the oven and let them sit for 5–10 minutes before turning out onto a wire rack. Serve immediately with lots of butter.

SWEETCORN, CHEDDAR AND JALAPEÑO MUFFIN

We created these muffins as a takeout version of our hugely popular jalapeño cornbread and they have now become a staple. The texture of these muffins is in your hands. We prefer them with a firm, dense consistency; resting the batter for up to 3 hours before baking will make them so. Cooking them straight away will make for a more crumbly, light-textured muffin. Either way they are delicious.

MAKES 12
430g plain flour
2 tsp baking powder
1½ tbsp smoked hot paprika
160g instant polenta
10g fine sea salt
3 eggs
400ml whole milk
240ml vegetable oil
320g sweetcorn kernels (tinned is fine)
160g Cheddar, grated
3 jalapeño peppers, deseeded and finely chopped
Handful of coriander (leaves and stalks), roughly chopped

1   Butter 12 individual muffin tins or a 12-hole muffin tin.

2   Sift the flour, baking powder and smoked paprika into a bowl. Add the polenta and salt and stir together until evenly mixed.

3   Lightly whisk the eggs in a large mixing bowl, before whisking in the milk and oil. The oil will rest on top, which is fine.

4   Mix the dry ingredients bowl into the wet and stir until combined, then fold in the sweetcorn, Cheddar, jalapeños and chopped coriander.

5   Divide the mixture evenly between the 12 muffin moulds and set aside – for a denser texture leave to rest in the moulds for 3 hours. When you are ready to bake, preheat the oven to 180°C.

6   Bake the muffins for 25–30 minutes. Check to see if they are ready by inserting a wooden skewer into the centre of a muffin. If the skewer comes out clean, they are ready. Remove from the oven and let them sit for 5–10 minutes before turning out on to a wire rack. Serve immediately.

BLUEBERRY AND LEMON FRIANDS WITH MAPLE MASCARPONE

The friand is an institution in New Zealand; you will find them in most cafés and coffee bars. They are mini oval cakes made with ground almonds and they have the most delicious texture. We have been making them with seasonal fruits and flavours since we first opened our doors, as they really do go so well with a coffee or tea – this recipe is one of our most popular versions. The maple mascarpone adds a decadent layer that you can choose to leave out – the friands are great on their own but we think the mascarpone takes them to another level.

MAKES 12
100g plain flour
250g caster sugar
135g ground almonds
165g butter, melted
Zest of 1 unwaxed lemon
1 tbsp lemon juice
5 egg whites
100g blueberries

MAPLE MASCARPONE
250g mascarpone
50g pure maple syrup
Zest of 1 unwaxed lemon
1 tsp lemon juice

1   Preheat the oven to 180°C and butter 12 × 100ml friand moulds. These are typically oval in shape but you could also use a regular muffin tin.

2   Combine the flour, sugar and ground almonds in a large bowl. Gently fold in the melted butter, lemon zest and juice.

3   In a stand mixer fitted with the whisk attachment, beat the egg whites to stiff peaks (or you can whisk by hand).

4   Gently mix the blueberries into the batter mixture.

5   Very gently fold a third of the egg whites into the mixture, then fold in half the remaining whites. Repeat the process with the last of the egg white. It is important the whites are mixed gently so the air is not knocked out of the batter, as this is what gives the friands their light fluffy texture.

6   Place a dollop of mixture without blueberries into the base of each mould. Then divide the remaining mixture evenly into the 12 moulds, making sure that the blueberries are evenly distributed.

7   Bake in the oven for 18–25 minutes. Check to see if they are ready by inserting a wooden skewer into the centre of a friand; if the skewer comes out clean, they are ready. Remove from the oven and allow to cool completely before turning out onto a wire rack.

8   Meanwhile, combine all the ingredients for the maple mascarpone together and chill until ready to use.

9   Once the friands have cooled completely, cut each one in half horizontally. Spoon a decent-sized dollop of maple mascarpone onto the base piece of each friand and then place the lid back on top.

NOTE

It is important that the friands are totally cool and the mascarpone is straight out of the fridge and firm. If the friands are still warm, the mascarpone will melt.

TAMARIND AND DATE MORNING BUN

The process for making these delicious brown balls of goodness takes some real commitment to get them just right, but the outcome is totally worth it.

It is a good idea to start these the day before you require them as proving times can vary and rushing the process can make for disappointing buns. You can even make these in advance by freezing the filled and rolled dough: just slice off what you need the day before and then prove the individual portions before baking first thing the next morning. We recommend eating them straight from the oven, when they are crisp on the outside and soft and gooey in the middle, but they are also great later on in the day as well.

MAKES 12
500g plain flour
75g caster sugar
250ml whole milk
15g fresh yeast (or use 7.5g dried yeast)
100g unsalted butter, softened
12g fine sea salt
250g unsalted butter, chilled
1 egg, beaten
1 tbsp honey
2 tbsp boiling water

TAMARIND AND DATE PURÉE
300g fresh or dried tamarind pods
100g Medjool dates
200ml boiling water

1 Place the flour, sugar, milk and yeast into a stand mixer fitted with the dough hook attachment and mix on slow speed for around 4–5 minutes to combine. Add the soft butter and continue to knead on slow until combined.

2 Now add the salt and knead on high speed for around 10 minutes until you can see a glossy sheen and the dough is elastic and has formed into a ball. Cover the bowl with a clean tea towel and leave to rest for 1 hour.

3 Remove the dough ball from the mixing bowl and use a rolling pin to roll into a rectangle 16cm wide and 30cm long. If the dough is a little sticky, use a very light dusting of flour on your work surface.

4 Now roll the chilled butter into a piece 15cm wide and 14cm long. Place the butter in the middle of the dough and fold the top and bottom of the dough into the centre. Spin the dough 90 degrees so the crease is now running vertically, and roll the dough out to a rectangle 16cm wide and 45cm long.

5 Fold the bottom edge of the rectangle up 5cm, then fold the top edge all the way down to meet it, then fold the dough in half. Move the dough onto a sheet of baking paper and rest in the fridge for 1 hour.

6 Remove from the fridge, roll out to a 16 × 45cm rectangle and then fold, then fold the bottom third up and the top third down over it. Move onto a sheet of baking paper again and return to the fridge to rest for 2 hours.

7 Meanwhile, make the tamarind and date purée. Place all the ingredients in a medium pan and bring up to the boil, then reduce the heat and simmer for about 5 minutes. Remove from the heat and drain away the water before pushing the mixture through a fine sieve – you should get about 150g purée. Set aside to cool while you grease 12 individual muffin tins or a 12-hole muffin tin with butter.

8   Remove the dough from the fridge and roll out to a 60 × 20cm rectangle. Spread the purée evenly over the dough and, starting at one of the short edges, roll up from top to bottom. Trim the edges and then cut the roll into 12 equal pieces. Place into the prepared tin and leave to prove until almost doubled in size. (This will depend on how warm your kitchen is, but could be from 3 to 6 hours).

9   Preheat the oven to 175°C. When the dough has doubled in size, brush the tops of the buns with egg wash and then bake in the oven for 15–20 minutes until golden. Leave to cool in the tin for 5–10 minutes. Combine the honey and boiling water in a small bowl.

10   Turn the buns out onto a wire rack with a tray underneath it and then brush the honey glaze over the top of each bun.

KIMCHI MORNING BUN

This recipe was inspired by a trip to San Francisco, where we encountered similar tasty little buns at a specialty coffee roastery, and it has become a staple on our takeout counters. It pays to start these the day before you need them due to proving times. The combination of savoury sweet pastry with tangy, spicy kimchi makes these a perfect bite for those who like something savoury in the morning (or afternoon!).

MAKES 12
500g plain flour
75g caster sugar
250ml whole milk
15g fresh yeast (or use 7.5g dried yeast)
100g unsalted butter, softened
12g fine sea salt
250g unsalted butter, chilled
400g Kimchi (see page 284 or use shop-bought)
1 egg, beaten
1 tbsp black sesame seeds

1   To make the dough for these buns follow steps 1–6 for the Tamarid and Date Morning Bun on the opposite page.

2   Lightly butter 12 individual muffins tins or a 12-hole muffin tin.

3   Roll out the dough to a 60 × 20cm rectangle. Spread the kimchi evenly over the dough and, starting at one of the short edges, roll up from top to bottom. Trim the edges and then cut the roll into 12 equal pieces. Place into the prepared tin or tins and leave to prove until almost doubled in size. (This will depend on how warm your kitchen is, but could be anything from 3 to 6 hours.)

4   Preheat the oven to 175°C. When the dough has doubled in size, brush the tops of the buns with egg wash and sprinkle the black sesame seeds evenly over the tops. Bake for 15–20 minutes.

5   Leave to cool in the tin for 5–10 minutes before turning out onto a wire rack. Enjoy on the day, while still a little warm!

BREAKFAST & BRUNCH

It all started with a cup of coffee and an egg (well, lots of eggs!). Weekday breakfasts and brunch at the weekends were a key part of what we wanted to offer at Caravan, and they are a serious passion of ours. As with great coffee, brunch is an institution in New Zealand and we wanted to bring that relaxed, easy-going, sunny Sunday experience to our London restaurants.

You can walk into our restaurants any morning of the week and see people sipping coffee and working on laptops or with papers out all over the tables. Breakfast meetings have become the new lunch meetings, and our spaces are filled with creatives, professionals, parents with kids and students from all walks of life, all enjoying coffee and breakfast.

For weekend brunches we like to take it up a couple of notches, largely due to the ever-increasing popularity of brunch in the UK. We turn the music up, and the food and coffee flow from morning to afternoon at a fun, energetic pace.

The breakfast section in this chapter includes easier, faster-paced recipes for workday breakfasts and quick and easy weekend dishes. As with our restaurant menus, there is a balance of healthy, energy-boosting ingredients with a few indulgent ones as well.

The brunch section was harder to compile as there are so many personal favourites and crowd-pleasers that we have built up over the years, some of which have been on our menus since day one. A few recipes may seem a bit complicated at first glance, but we urge you to give them a go. Cooking brunch at home for friends and family is one of our most pleasing weekend activities and turning it into a lengthy feast makes it all the more enjoyable. Do some of the preparation the day before so you can enjoy more time chatting to your loved ones – many components yield better results when cooked the day before anyway. Start off with Bloody Marys or a breakfast martini (depending on how you want the day to roll!), a preamble of fruit or avocado on toast and then let the feasting begin.

OAT, SUPER SEED, FRUIT AND NUT GRANOLA WITH SALTED COCONUT YOGHURT

We love this granola. It has been on all our menus, and our customers seem to love the flavours and the fact that it's packed full of slow-release deliciousness to set you up for the day ahead. Don't be bound by the fruits, nuts or seeds listed here; feel free to sub in any of your favourites to create your own delicious version. The key ratio is the oats to liquid so they are not greasy but all lightly coated. The salt on top is optional but we highly recommend you try it. It lifts the whole dish to the next level.

MAKES 850G

100g good-quality honey (we use New Zealand Manuka)
100g coconut oil
30g coconut palm sugar
5 cardamom pods, bashed
500g organic jumbo oats
50g desiccated coconut
50g raw buckwheat
20g sesame seeds
50g pumpkin seeds
30g chia seeds
20g milled flaxseeds (optional)
50g shelled pistachio nuts, toasted
50g dried cranberries
50g dried goji berries (optional)
150g dried apricots, cut into thirds

TO SERVE (PER PERSON)

40g coconut yoghurt
Pinch of flaked sea salt
1 tsp bee pollen (optional)
Unsweetened almond milk (or other milk of choice)

1   Preheat the oven to 170°C.

2   Combine the honey, coconut oil, coconut palm sugar and cardamom pods together in a small pan and gently heat to dissolve the sugar and honey.

3   In a large bowl, combine the oats, coconut, buckwheat, sesame seeds, pumpkin seeds, chia seeds, flaxseeds and pistachio nuts.

4   Place a sieve over the large bowl and strain the honey mixture through the sieve to remove the cardamom pods. Mix the honey mixture through the oats, making sure all the oats and other dry ingredients are thoroughly covered.

5   Transfer the mixture to 2 large baking trays and spread out to create a shallow layer on each tray. Bake in the oven for 40–50 minutes, stirring every 10 minutes or so.

6   Remove from the oven and allow to cool fully before mixing in the dried fruits and storing in an airtight jar. This will keep in a cool dry place for up to 2 months.

7   Serve each 90g portion of granola with a dollop of coconut yoghurt, a pinch of flaked sea salt and the bee pollen, if using. Add almond milk to taste.

OVERNIGHT MUESLI

I have always loved overnight or bircher muesli, but for some reason never made it that much. However, as life has got steadily busier juggling kids and the businesses, I now make this often because it's so quick and easy for a weekday breakfast as it's prepared the night before. It's also one of the best healthy, fast breakfast options around, and the possibilities are endless with the ingredients you can add to the mix. For a dairy-free option, milk can be replaced with apple juice or nut milks and the yoghurt can be subbed out for a dairy-free yoghurt. You can also add fresh fruit or seeds before serving – banana, blueberries and pumpkin seeds work brilliantly. (LHH)

SERVES 4
160g rolled oats
50g buckwheat flakes
1 tbsp flaxseeds
1 tbsp chia seeds
1 apple, grated
1 pear, grated
1 tbsp lemon juice
50g pitted Medjool dates, chopped
50g raisins
50g honey or maple syrup
480ml whole milk
340g natural yoghurt

TO SERVE
Toasted pumpkin or sunflower seeds
Toasted flaked almonds
Fresh fruit
Rice bran, wheatgerm or superfood
powder (optional)

1   Place all the ingredients into a large bowl and mix well to combine. Cover the bowl and chill in the fridge overnight.

2   In the morning, spoon into breakfast bowls and serve topped with whatever you have to hand that takes your fancy – toasted seeds or nuts work well, as do seasonal fruits such as bananas, strawberries or blueberries. Stirring a teaspoon of rice bran, wheatgerm or a sprouted grain powder will add some extra nutrients and fibre!

SESAME LABNEH WITH FRESH SEASONAL FRUIT, CHIA-HONEY SYRUP AND CACAO NIBS

This is a very simple fruit salad recipe with the added goodness of sesame, chia, honey and cacao nibs. In the restaurants we use a combination of three seasonal fruits, and we change it regularly. We look for a good balance of crunch, flavour and texture. You can use whatever you have available and takes your fancy. Substitute the Labneh for straight-up Greek yoghurt or for dairy-free coconut yoghurt if you like. Smashed, toasted walnuts or pumpkin seeds are a great addition as well.

SERVES 1
250g Greek yoghurt
50g tahini
3g flaked sea salt

CHIA-HONEY SYRUP
60ml water
100ml honey
1½ tbsp chia seeds

TO SERVE (PER PERSON)
150g fresh seasonal fruit, chopped
into bite-sized pieces
10g cacao nibs

1   First make the labneh. Place a piece of muslin or cheesecloth into a bowl, allowing the fabric to drape over the edges of the bowl. Pour in the Greek yoghurt. Bring the corners of the cloth together and tie with a piece of string.

2   Hang the yoghurt, in the cloth, over a bowl for 1½–2 hours. The bowl will catch the drips as the moisture is squeezed from the yoghurt. You can hang the yoghurt from the tap in your kitchen sink, with the bowl below, or hang it in the fridge overnight if you want a really thick labneh.

3   Meanwhile, make the chia-honey syrup. Gently heat the water and honey in a small pan to dissolve the honey. Place the chia seeds in a small bowl, pour the warm syrup over them and allow to stand for at least 1 hour until the seeds are puffy and look like black pearls. This will keep in an airtight container in the fridge for 3–4 days.

4   Once the yoghurt has thickened, remove it from the cloth and place in a bowl. If you want it thicker, you can give it a tight squeeze with your hands to release more moisture. Mix in the tahini and salt. If you are not using the labneh straight away, store it in an airtight container in the fridge – it will keep for 3–5 days.

5   To assemble, dollop the labneh in the bottom of a bowl and spread it out with the back of a spoon, leaving a well in the middle. Top with the fresh fruit, spoon over 2 tablespoons of the chia-honey syrup and then sprinkle over the cacao nibs.

AVOCADO WITH CHILLI FLAKES AND LEMON ON GRANARY TOAST

This exact recipe was on our very first breakfast and all-day brunch menus, and it has never left due to its popularity as a simple, nutritional, full-of-flavour basic. It is perhaps the simplest dish in the book to prepare but it relies on a number of factors to take it from being mediocre to great. You must choose great bread – seek out your local artisan baker and source a multigrain or sourdough. The avocado must be perfectly ripe, soft and not at all discoloured. The olive oil must be good-quality and the chilli flakes need to be soft and palatable. If you want to pimp your avocado on toast up a bit go crazy and add a poached or soft-boiled egg.

SERVES 4
4 ripe avocados (not brown or discoloured)
3 tbsp extra-virgin olive oil, plus extra for drizzling
2 tsp flaked sea salt
1 tbsp lemon juice
Cracked black pepper
4 slices of granary bread (or whatever you prefer)
1 tbsp chilli flakes (we use Aleppo but use what you have)

1   Cut the avocados in half around the stone and spoon the fruit into a mixing bowl. Gently mash the avocado with a fork until it is a mixture of some large chunks and some more mashed avocado.

2   Add the olive oil, sea salt, lemon juice and pepper and stir gently to combine.

3   Meanwhile toast the 4 slices of bread.

4   Spoon the avocado mixture onto each slice of toast and sprinkle with the chilli flakes. Drizzle a little more olive oil over the top.

OAT AND QUINOA PORRIDGE WITH BANANA, DATES, MAPLE SYRUP AND ALMONDS

I grew up on porridge for breakfast. My Dad would make it and my option for garnish was either brown sugar or a spoonful of honey. Mostly I went for honey, which meant a spoonful of firm Manuka honey was placed in the bowl and the hot porridge poured on top. In time, the honey would melt so it became soft enough that I could lift the spoon out and drizzle the honey over the porridge – for me this is a magical childhood food memory.

This is our go-to porridge recipe for the colder months. When making this at home you can keep the base of the recipe the same and then play around with other ingredients when seasonality calls. Try swapping the maple syrup for raw honey, for example, or the dates for fresh raspberries or blueberries. I'm also a sucker for replacing the almond milk with milk and cream. (MK)

SERVES 4
100g quinoa (we use red)
600ml unsweetened almond milk, plus extra for serving
200g jumbo oats
¼ tsp fine sea salt
100ml maple syrup
2 bananas, roughly chopped
8 pitted Medjool dates, torn in half
2 tbsp flaked almonds, toasted

1   Bring 300ml water to the boil in a pan and add the quinoa. Simmer for 12–15 minutes until soft. Drain off the water, and set aside to cool. (You can do this in advance – the quinoa will keep for 3 days in the fridge.)

2   Gently heat the almond milk in a small pan, add the oats and the quinoa and bring to a gentle simmer. Cook for about 4–5 minutes until the almond milk has been absorbed and the oats are soft to the bite. Add the salt and stir to combine.

3   Pour in the maple syrup and turn the mixture over to create a ripple effect with the maple syrup, then pour straight into the serving bowls. Top with the banana and the dates then finally sprinkle over the flaked almonds. Serve with a jug of almond milk.

CHEDDAR AND CARAWAY ONION JAM ON SOURDOUGH TOAST

This seemingly basic dish gained far more attention on our menus than we ever expected. The three components are equally as important: the toast must be perfect sourdough; the Cheddar must be full of flavour – soft in the middle with a hard, caramelised crust; and the onions in the jam have to be caramelised properly. Bring these three things together and you have a winning dish for any time of the day. The great news is the onion jam can be made in advance and stored in the fridge for up to 3 weeks, making this a super easy and fast dish to pull together.

SERVES 4
4 slices of good-quality sourdough
60g mature Cheddar, grated
Small handful of chopped chives
or parsley (optional)

CARAWAY ONION JAM
60ml vegetable oil
4 medium white onions, sliced
(about 500g)
4 medium red onions, sliced
(about 500g)
½ tsp salt
1 tsp caraway seeds, toasted
250ml red wine vinegar (we use
Cabernet Sauvignon vinegar)
110g light muscovado sugar
¼ tsp cracked black pepper

1   First make the jam. Gently heat the oil in a medium pan and add the onions and salt. Keeping the heat low, cover the pan with a lid and let the onions cook for about 10 minutes until they have fully softened with some liquid around them.

2   Increase the heat and bring the liquid to a boil, allowing it to reduce and begin caramelisation. Once the onions start to colour, continue cooking over a medium heat, stirring regularly, so that they brown but do not catch and burn.

3   Once the onions have turned brown in colour and the oil is beginning to separate from the onion, add the caraway seeds and fry for a couple of minutes. Add the vinegar, sugar and pepper and cook to reduce the liquid and dissolve the sugar.

4   Once the contents of the pan are dark brown and glossy with no liquid bleeding from them, remove from the heat and cool. This recipe will make more onion jam than you need for 4 slices of toast but it will keep in a sterilised jar in the fridge for up to 3 weeks.

5   To assemble the dish, toast the sourdough slices while you preheat the grill to high. Put the toast on a baking tray and evenly distribute the grated Cheddar. Put the toast under the grill until the cheese is completely melted, but not browning.

6   Remove from the grill and spread about 3 tablespoons of onion jam over the top of the melted cheese on each slice. Return to the grill until the cheese is just starting to brown. Serve immediately, scattered with some chopped chives or parsley if you fancy a bit of green.

CREAMY SOY MUSHROOMS ON SOURDOUGH TOAST

When I was a kid, mushrooms on toast were a regular feature on the weekly food calendar, generally at Sunday brunch time. They were more often than not served with lamb's kidneys too. I remember smothering the kidneys in as much sauce as I could to hide their taste. These days, I have my mushrooms neat, except for the cream and soy sauce that is.

These mushrooms started life in our kitchen as a component of the Caravan Fry. But within days of opening, we were getting requests for the mushrooms as sides and just as a dish on their own, with toast. They are the reason the 'on toast' section of our menu was born. They also don't take too long to prepare and require only minimal effort for a seriously delicious mushroom dish. (MK)

SERVES 4

160g unsalted butter
2 medium brown onions (about 240g), finely diced
3 garlic cloves, finely chopped
400g chestnut mushrooms, roughly chopped
200ml double cream
2 tbsp red wine vinegar
20ml light soy sauce
2 tbsp chopped parsley, plus extra to garnish
4 slices of good-quality sourdough
Butter for spreading

1   Melt the butter in a medium pan and cook the onions and garlic over a medium-low heat for 3–4 minutes until they are soft and translucent.

2   Add the chestnut mushrooms and cook over a medium heat for 8–10 minutes until the liquid starts to seep from the mushrooms. Increase the heat slightly to reduce the mushroom liquid by half, being careful not to caramelise the mushrooms.

3   Add the cream and reduce by three-quarters, then add the red wine vinegar and soy sauce and continue to reduce until thick but still runny enough to soak into your toast. Stir through the chopped parsley.

4   Toast the sourdough and butter each slice generously. Top with the soy mushrooms and garnish with a little more chopped parsley. Enjoy immediately.

COCONUT BREAD WITH LEMON CURD CREAM CHEESE AND POACHED RHUBARB

When I was growing up in New Zealand, I used to love the coconut bread made by one of the stallholders at the Polynesian market in Newtown. This version is not exactly what I used to eat but it's pretty close. It's delicious on its own, but we have created a pretty special sweet brunch dish with lemon curd cream cheese and poached rhubarb. When rhubarb is out of season or not at its best, we use strawberries or other delicious seasonal fruit. (MK)

SERVES 6–8
COCONUT BREAD (MAKES 1 LOAF)
360g plain flour
1½ tsp baking powder
1½ tsp salt
180g caster sugar
135g desiccated coconut
3 eggs
1½ tsp vanilla extract
60ml whole milk
240ml coconut milk

LEMON CURD CREAM CHEESE
60g unsalted butter
130g caster sugar
Zest of 2 unwaxed lemons
120ml lemon juice
2 eggs, lightly whisked
2 egg yolks, lightly whisked
100g cream cheese,
at room temperature

POACHED RHUBARB
300g unrefined caster sugar
4 tbsp lemon juice
1 vanilla pod, split lengthways
and seeds scraped out
400g rhubarb, trimmed and chopped
into 8cm sections
Butter, for frying

1   First make the bread. Preheat the oven to 170°C and line a 23 × 13 × 7cm loaf tin with baking paper.

2   In a large mixing bowl, combine the flour, baking powder, salt, sugar and coconut. In a separate bowl combine the eggs, vanilla extract, milk and coconut milk, whisking lightly to break up and mix eggs.

3   Combine the wet ingredients with the dry ingredients and mix lightly until you have a smooth batter. Pour into the lined loaf tin and bake in the oven for 45 minutes until golden brown on top. Check whether the loaf is cooked by inserting a wooden skewer into the centre; if it comes out clean, the bread is cooked. Remove the cooked loaf from the oven and turn out onto a wire rack to cool.

4   To make the lemon curd cream cheese, gently heat the butter, sugar, lemon zest and juice together in a pan until the butter has melted and the sugar dissolved. Whisk the eggs and egg yolks together in a small bowl and then pour into the pan, whisking over a gentle heat until thick and creamy. Remove from the heat, pass through a sieve and set aside to cool. Once cool, whisk the cream cheese through the lemon curd and then chill in the fridge until needed.

5   To make the poached rhubarb, put the sugar, lemon juice and vanilla seeds and pod into a small pan with 300ml water and place over a medium heat until the sugar has dissolved. Add the rhubarb to the pan and increase the heat. As soon as it comes to the boil turn off the heat and cover with a lid. Leave to sit for 15 minutes, then transfer to a container to cool, with the vanilla pod. (This can be stored in the fridge for up to 1 week.)

6   Slice the coconut bread into thick slices (about 2.5cm) while you melt some butter in a large frying pan. Add the bread slices, a couple at a time, and fry on one side for around 3 minutes until golden brown. Flip to the other side and continue frying until golden brown.

7   Transfer the coconut bread to individual plates. Top each slice with some of the lemon curd cream cheese and 4 pieces of rhubarb.

GRAIN PANCAKE WITH MAPLE SYRUP AND BUTTER

Inspired by the many and varied grain pancakes we ate while travelling the length of the west coast of America, this is our version. There were definitely highs and lows on our grain pancake journey, and much discussion as to which grains had gone into the ones we loved. But we all agreed that a great grain pancake is hard to beat, especially as a healthier breakfast option. There is a lot of good stuff packed into these pancakes, creating a much more textured, moist and flavourful result. It might seem like a bit of an effort getting all these ingredients out, but trust us – it is worth it. As with most pancakes, maple syrup is the perfect companion, especially when paired with a dollop of melting butter.

MAKES 1 LARGE PANCAKE
OR 6–8 SMALLER ONES
80g wholemeal spelt flour
60g instant polenta
30g buckwheat flour
30g rye flour
20g rolled oats
30g muscovado sugar
1 tbsp milled flaxseeds (optional)
1 tbsp poppy seeds
1 tsp fine sea salt
1½ tsp bicarbonate of soda
3 eggs
400ml buttermilk
100g unsalted butter, melted
125g cooked brown rice (optional)
Butter, for frying

1   Preheat the oven to 175°C.

2   Combine all the dry ingredients in a large bowl and whisk to remove lumps.

3   In another large bowl, gently whisk the eggs, buttermilk and butter together.

4   Mix the dry ingredients into the wet until well combined. Finally fold in the cooked brown rice, if using.

5   Melt a little butter in a heavy-based ovenproof pan and spoon about 100ml of batter into the pan. Cook on one side, then place the pan in the oven for around 10 minutes or until brown on the underside and some bubbles have formed on the surface. This will make it a lot easier to flip. To make individual pancakes, use 120ml (about half a cup) of batter per portion.

6   Remove from the oven, flip the pancake over and cook the other side until nicely browned.

7   Ideally serve the pancake as soon as it is cooked, on a large board cut into pieces with maple syrup and butter dolloped on top.

AUBERGINE PURÉE WITH PRESERVED LEMON GREMOLATA AND POACHED EGGS

If you love aubergine, you will love this brunch dish. It's great to serve as an alternative to meaty, gluten-heavy recipes and the flavours are wonderfully complementary. As with many brunch dishes, the eggs are key, and we often get asked how we get our poached eggs to look the way they do. We have included a dedicated recipe for poached eggs to help you achieve the same results (see page 86). This dish also goes very well with chargrilled merguez sausage or chorizo too. The aubergine purée and gremolata is absolutely delicious with crispbread as a starter.

SERVES 4
8 poached eggs (see page 86)
Sourdough toast or grilled pitta, to serve

AUBERGINE PURÉE
2 aubergines
1 garlic clove, minced
Zest and juice of 1 unwaxed lemon
Small handful of flat-leaf parsley, roughly chopped
50g tahini
40ml olive oil
50g Greek yoghurt
Sea salt and black pepper

PRESERVED LEMON, CHILLI AND SUMAC GREMOLATA
1 tbsp Preserved Lemon rind (see page 285 or use shop-bought), diced
1 tbsp sesame seeds, toasted
2 tbsp roughly chopped flat-leaf parsley
½ tsp sumac
1 tsp chilli flakes

1   Preheat the oven 200°C.

2   Prick the aubergines with a skewer, place in a roasting dish and roast until soft all the way through, about 30–35 minutes.

3   Halve the aubergines, scoop out the flesh and place in a colander to allow to drain and cool. When cool, roughly chop.

4   Combine all the remaining ingredients in a medium bowl and season with salt and pepper. Add the chopped aubergine and stir to combine.

5   Meanwhile, combine all the gremolata ingredients in a small bowl.

6   To bring the dish together, spread the aubergine purée into a serving dish and sprinkle the gremolata over the top. Place the poached eggs on top. Serve with sourdough or grain toast or, even better, Greek pitta bread, brushed with water and oil and then grilled.

CORNBREAD FRENCH TOAST WITH AVOCADO, BACON AND PAPRIKA MAPLE SYRUP

Turning our staple cornbread into French toast was a stroke of genius from Miles and his kitchen team. The texture and flavour of the cornbread makes for a much more exciting and interesting version of French toast, and it pairs so well with the fresh flavour of the avocado and salty-sweet bacon and maple combo. This dish has been one of the biggest sellers on our brunch menu since we opened the doors in 2010, and it is likely to remain in one form or another for many years to come. Make the cornbread the day before and you'll have a great, easy brunch option to enjoy with friends. (CA)

SERVES 4
3 eggs
90ml whole milk
90ml double cream
Butter, for frying
8 slices of Cornbread (see page 87)
12 slices of streaky bacon
100ml maple syrup
1 tsp hot smoked paprika
1 ripe avocado, sliced (or use the Avocado with Chilli Flakes and Lemon on page 56)

1   Preheat the oven to 180°C.

2   Whisk together the eggs, milk and cream until combined and pour into a flat, shallow dish.

3   Melt a knob of butter in a large frying pan over a medium heat while you place slices of cornbread into the dish so they get drowned in the egg mixture. When the butter has melted and is turning golden brown, place 4 slices of cornbread into the pan. Fry the soused cornbread on one side for a couple of minutes until brown then flip over to brown the other side.

4   Remove the French toast from the pan and place on a baking tray and then repeat with the remaining bread slices and egg mixture. Put the tray of cornbread into the oven and cook for 5 minutes.

5   Meanwhile grill or fry the streaky bacon until crisp. Put the maple syrup and paprika into a small pan and bring to the boil, then set aside.

6   To bring the dish together, arrange 2 slices of cornbread French toast on each plate. Top with sliced avocado (or a dollop of dressed avocado) and 3 slices of cooked streaky bacon. Drizzle over the paprika maple syrup and serve.

BAKED EGGS WITH TOMATO-PEPPER RAGOUT AND GREEK YOGHURT

When I first arrived in London I worked with an Israeli pastry chef, and on special occasions he would make a version of this for staff breakfast. It was a joy to behold and a great way to start the day. He would talk about Dr Shakshuka in a food market in Tel Aviv who, when he prepared a pan of this, would sell out within minutes of it being ready. We sell a lot of our version of baked eggs, and I always make it when on holiday with groups of friends. It's so easy and everyone will think you are a pro when you pull it off. This is a great dish in its own right, but adding chargrilled merguez or chorizo sausage gives it a wonderful meaty lift. (MK)

SERVES 4–6
2 tsp coriander seeds
4 tsp cumin seeds
2 tsp mustard seeds
250ml olive oil (it seems like
a lot, but it is needed)
1 large white onion, roughly diced
5 garlic cloves, sliced
2 red peppers, deseeded and
roughly chopped
10 tomatoes, cored and roughly
chopped (we use large beefsteak)
8 eggs
200g thick Greek yoghurt
Handful of flat-leaf parsley leaves
Pinch of chilli flakes (we
use Aleppo)
Pinch of sumac
Sea salt and black pepper
Toasted pitta, Turkish flatbread or
sourdough, to serve

1   Preheat the oven to 180°C. Meanwhile, in a large, heavy-based ovenproof pan (at least 30cm in diameter), dry toast the coriander seeds over a low heat (ensure you keep the pan moving at all times when toasting spices). When they are golden and fragrant, use a pestle and mortar to grind them to a coarse powder.

2   Add the cumin and mustard seeds to the pan and toast over a low heat as before. Add the olive oil, ground coriander seeds and chopped onion to the pan and stir to infuse the oil with all the flavours. Cook until the onion softens, about 10–15 minutes.

3   Add the garlic, turn up the heat and cook hard, stirring frequently, until the onion starts to brown around the edges. Now add the chopped peppers and cook until they are soft, about 15 minutes. Next drop in the tomatoes and cook over a medium heat until the tomatoes collapse and have bled all their juices. Simmer and reduce the juice until you have a thick, shiny sauce and then season to taste with salt and pepper.

4   Use the back of a spoon to rough up the surface of the sauce. Break the eggs into the dips in the sauce, making sure they are evenly spaced. Simmer until the tomato sauce bubbles up between the eggs and the whites of the egg begin to cook, then place the pan in the oven and bake for around 10 minutes. (You can also cook this dish on top of the stove. Just put a lid on the pan once the whites of the eggs start to cook. You want to achieve cooked whites and runny yolks. You will need to turn the sauce over or gently pull the eggs apart with a spoon to reveal uncooked egg whites. This will ensure the hot sauce will cook the whites before the yolks harden. Do this every couple of minutes and gently so as not to break the yolks.) Remove the pan from the oven and leave to stand for a few minutes – this will allow all the delicious oil to rise to the top.

5   Garnish the eggs with dollops of Greek yoghurt, parsley leaves, chilli flakes and sumac and serve with toasted pitta, flatbread or sourdough.

CRAB OMELETTE WITH CITRUS MAYONNAISE

This is one of our favourite brunch omelettes, and the crab adds a great dimension to the dish. Brown crabmeat can polarise opinion and if you are a fan, you should feel free to include some, though we have specified white here. If you are wondering what to do with any brown crabmeat you don't wish to use in the omelette, try cooking it out slowly with fish sauce and palm sugar until it becomes a super funky, crab-flavoured caramel paste. It is amazing for seasoning curries, soups and sauces.

SERVES 2
3 large eggs
2 large egg yolks
25ml whole milk
75ml double cream
½ tbsp light soy sauce
½ tsp ground turmeric
25g unsalted butter
150g white crabmeat
3 tbsp finely chopped coriander
4 spring onions, thinly sliced
1 lemon, cut into wedges
4 tbsp Citrus Mayonnaise
(see page 274)

1 Preheat the oven 170°C.

2 Put the eggs, egg yolks, milk, cream, soy sauce and turmeric in a large bowl and mix to combine.

3 Heat the butter in a large, heavy-based ovenproof pan. Add the egg mixture and using a wooden spoon or spatula, pull the mixture into the middle, allowing the vacant hot pan space to be re-filled with raw egg mixture. Do this 4 or 5 times.

4 Cook for 2 minutes until just beginning to brown around the edges, then evenly distribute the crabmeat, coriander and spring onions over the top, retaining some coriander and sliced spring onion to garnish.

5 Place the pan in the oven and cook for 10–12 minutes until the middle is firm to the touch. Remove from the oven and use a spatula to transfer to a serving board or large plate.

6 Garnish with the reserved spring onion and chopped coriander, and spoon the citrus mayonnaise on top.

SHRIMP 'N' GRITS WITH BOURBON BUTTER

When we first opened Caravan, we wanted the menu to be truly 'well travelled', drawing inspiration from our New Zealand roots, but also our global eating sessions over the years. One of our obsessions back then was southern American soul food and so we created our own version of the classic shrimp 'n' grits. Grits are a southern American classic with Native American origins. Just like polenta, grits are made from coarsely ground corn. The main difference between the two is the variety of corn used in its production. Although the recipe below is not strictly a recipe for grits, but rather a creamy white polenta, the foundation and influence of the dish is the same, and this creamy cornmeal porridge is a great vehicle for the shrimp and bourbon.

SERVES 4
SHRIMP BUTTER
2 tbsp olive oil
2 shallots, halved and sliced
2 garlic cloves, sliced
1 tsp ground nutmeg
½ tsp cayenne pepper
80ml bourbon, plus ½ tbsp
for serving
125g unsalted butter
200g brown shrimp, peeled
Zest and juice of 1 unwaxed
lemon, plus extra zest
to garnish
Small handful of flat-leaf
parsley, finely chopped

GRITS (CREAMY POLENTA)
300ml whole milk
300ml double cream
75g butter
1 thyme sprig
1 bay leaf
100g white polenta
60g crème fraîche
½ tsp fine sea salt

1   Heat the olive oil in a medium frying pan and add the shallots and garlic. Cook, stirring, over a medium heat for 6–8 minutes until browned.

2   Stir through the nutmeg and cayenne and cook over a low heat for 2–3 minutes. Deglaze the pan with the bourbon and stir as the liquid reduces and thickens. Add the butter and stir through to melt, then add the shrimp, lemon zest and juice and stir through. Set aside while you prepare the grits.

3   Put the milk, cream, butter, thyme and bay leaf into a medium pan, place over a medium heat and bring to the boil.

4   Remove the pan from the heat and pour in the polenta. Stir to combine then return to a gentle heat, stirring continuously until the liquid thickens and the polenta is cooked – this should take around 5–6 minutes. Remove from the heat and add the crème fraîche and salt. Pour the grits into a serving dish.

5   Return the shrimp to the heat and add the remaining half tablespoon of bourbon. Spoon the shrimp over the grits and sprinkle with the finely chopped parsley and lemon zest.

FRIED BROWN RICE WITH BRUSSELS SPROUTS, FRIED EGGS, GREENS AND CHILLI

Whenever we cook brown rice, we always do a bit too much, just so we can fry the leftovers for breakfast. It's really important for this recipe that the rice has been well drained and completely cooled to ensure you get those delicious crispy grains of rice. The mustard greens can happily be replaced with kimchi or another leafy green such as chard, spinach or kale. You can use wok water to provide steam for cooking vegetables – as the steam is produced, the water evaporates to leave the full flavour of the soy and vinegar. It's a handy thing to have in the fridge, and will keep for a long time. This is a seriously full-of-flavour brunch dish that we have enjoyed many times with friends at home.

SERVES 4–6
6 tbsp rapeseed oil
150g brown onions, thinly sliced
300g Brussels sprouts, sliced
800g cooked brown rice
5 spring onions, thinly sliced
200g mustard greens, kimchi or
spring greens
6–8 eggs, fried
Handful of coriander, roughly chopped
100g peanuts, roughly chopped
6 lime wedges
Fried Shallots (optional, see page 288)

CHILLI PASTE
50g fresh ginger, peeled and
roughly chopped
4 garlic cloves
Small handful of coriander (leaves
and stalks), roughly chopped
3 red chillies, roughly chopped
2 tbsp rapeseed oil

WOK WATER
100ml water
50ml light soy sauce
50ml Chinese black vinegar (optional)

1   Put all the chilli paste ingredients into a food processor and blend to a paste. Transfer to a small bowl and set aside.

2   Next make the wok water. Combine all the ingredients in a bowl and set aside.

3   Heat a tablespoon of the oil in a large frying pan and fry the onions over a medium heat until browned, about 10 minutes. Remove from the pan and transfer to a large bowl. Add another tablespoon of oil to the pan and fry the Brussels sprouts in the same way, then transfer to the bowl with the onions.

4   Adding a tablespoon of oil to the frying pan for each batch, fry a quarter of the rice over a high heat with a quarter of the paste for 3–4 minutes. Then add 50ml wok water to the pan and allow this to reduce by half. Remove from the pan and add to the bowl with the onions and sprouts. Keep this bowl covered with a piece of foil to keep it warm. Repeat with the remaining three batches of rice, adding the spring onions and mustard greens at the end on the last batch to heat them through.

5   Transfer the fried rice, onions and sprouts to a serving dish and top with 6–8 fried eggs. Scatter over the coriander, peanuts, lime wedges and fried shallots and serve in the centre of the table for guests to help themselves.

SALT BEEF FRITTERS, GREEN BEANS AND FRIED EGGS

Salt beef for dinner – served with mustard sauce, boiled potatoes and carrots – is something we all grew up with in New Zealand, and it invariably meant leftovers. These would be transformed into lunch the following day in the form of a salt beef sandwich or salad with mustard and relishes. My favourite use for leftover salt beef, however, is to turn it into these delicious fritters. If you make the batter for these the night before, the flavour of the beef infiltrates the fritters more. The fritters themselves make for a delicious base for the beans, mustard and egg. (MK)

SERVES 4
2 tbsp olive oil
8 eggs

SALT BEEF
1kg salted brisket (you can get this from any good butcher)
100g golden syrup
1 onion, halved
1 carrot, halved lengthways
1 celery stick
2 bay leaves
120ml apple cider vinegar
10 peppercorns

FRITTERS
200g plain flour
1½ tsp baking powder
2 eggs
100ml whole milk
½ tbsp English mustard
50g Greek yoghurt
25g unsalted butter, melted
Large handful of flat-leaf parsley, roughly chopped
2 tbsp finely chopped chives
1 tsp fine sea salt
½ tsp cracked black pepper
4 tbsp rapeseed oil, for frying

GREEN BEANS
300g green beans, trimmed
2 tbsp raw honey
2 tbsp red wine vinegar (preferably Cabernet Sauvignon)
2 tbsp English mustard
1 tsp fine sea salt
½ tsp cracked black pepper
60ml mustard oil
60ml olive oil
Large handful of flat-leaf parsley, roughly chopped

1   First prepare the salt beef. Place all the ingredients into a large pan and add enough cold water to cover (about 2 litres). Bring to the boil and then reduce the heat, cover with a lid and simmer for about 6 hours until completely tender.

2   Remove the pan from the heat and leave the beef to cool in the liquid. Once cool, discard the cooking liquid and finely chop or shred the beef. Set aside while you make the fritter batter.

3   Place the flour and baking powder in a large mixing bowl and make a well in the centre. Mix in the eggs with a wooden spoon. Add the milk, mustard, yoghurt and butter and stir to form a thick batter.

4   Add 450g of the cooked and shredded salt beef (any left over will keep for up to 4 days in the fridge), the parsley, chives, salt and pepper and stir through. Set the batter aside until ready to cook.

5   Meanwhile prepare the green beans. Bring a large pan of salted water to the boil and drop in the beans. Maintain a rolling boil for 3 minutes then drain the beans and refresh in cold water. Set aside.

6   Put the honey, vinegar, mustard, salt and pepper in a large mixing bowl and whisk to combine. Combine the oils in a pouring jug and then add to the bowl, whisking continuously until the dressing emulsifies and thickens. Just before serving, pour half the dressing over the green beans and scatter with the chopped parsley.

7   To cook the fritters, heat the oil in a pan and when hot, spoon a ladleful (about 75ml) of the mixture into the hot oil and fry on both sides until golden brown. Depending on the size of your pan, you should be able to cook a couple of fritters at a time. Remove from the pan and drain on kitchen paper, then keep warm in a low oven while you cook the rest of the fritters. Continue until all the batter is used up – you should get 8–12 fritters.

8   Now fry the eggs: heat the oil in a large non-stick pan until hot.
    Break in the eggs one at a time – you should be able to fry 3–4 in the
    pan at a time but take care not to overcrowd. The oil needs to be
    hot enough so that when you crack the eggs into the pan, the white
    immediately starts to set and does not run too much. Cook the eggs
    over a medium heat until the edges are crispy and brown.

9   To bring the dish together, place 2 or 3 fritters on each plate. Top
    the fritters with 2 fried eggs per serving and season with salt and
    pepper. Place the dressed green beans to the side of the fritters and
    drizzle the remaining dressing over the top of the dish.

HAM HOCK HASH WITH POACHED EGGS, PEAS AND HOLLANDAISE

This is a great dish to serve if you are having a crew round for brunch as you can do a lot of the preparation the day before. The ham hock is almost better the following day, and as it takes 3–4 hours to prepare, it definitely pays to have this part prepared in advance. The smashed peas can also be prepped ahead of time, but do not add the vinegar to the peas until just before serving as it will discolour them. If you add it last minute, they will stay a vibrant green colour. We serve this dish as individual mini hashes at the restaurants, crumbed and fried, and the combination of flavours never fails to satisfy.

SERVES 6
HAM HOCK HASH
2 smoked ham hocks
1 carrot
2 brown onions
1 tsp black peppercorns
1 tsp whole allspice berries
800g peeled Desiree potatoes
2 tbsp vegetable oil
2 leeks, thinly sliced
Handful of flat-leaf parsley,
roughly chopped
2 tbsp English mustard
6 poached eggs (see page 86)

SMASHED PEAS
120g frozen or fresh peas
2 spring onions, thinly sliced
Small handful of flat-leaf
parsley, torn or roughly chopped
Small handful of mint leaves,
roughly chopped
½ tsp fine sea salt
½ tsp cracked black pepper
100ml olive oil
1 tbsp apple cider vinegar

HOLLANDAISE
(make this up to 1 hour ahead
and keep in a covered bowl
at room temperature)
3 egg yolks
1 tbsp lemon juice
½ tsp fine sea salt
250g unsalted butter, melted

1   Put the hocks, carrot, one of the onions (cut in half), peppercorns and allspice berries into a large pan and cover with about 2 litres of cold water. Bring to the boil then turn down the heat and cover with a lid. Maintain a gentle simmer for about 3 hours or until the bone pulls out from the meat with ease. Keep an eye on it while it simmers; you may need to top the pan up with water to keep the hock covered.

2   Once cooked, remove the hocks from the pan, allow to cool a little then pick off the meat, discarding the fat and bone. Set aside.

3   Now prepare the smashed peas. Cook the peas in a large pan of boiling well-salted water for 2 minutes. Drain and refresh in cold water. Drain again and tip the peas into a food processor. Add the spring onions, parsley, mint, salt and pepper and pulse until the peas are broken up but not puréed. Transfer to a small bowl and add the olive oil; mix together with a spoon. Stir in the vinegar just before serving.

4   Preheat the oven to 180°C.

5   Cut the potatoes into quarters, add to a large pan and cover with water. Bring to the boil and cook until the potatoes are just soft, about10–15 minutes. Drain and then tip them onto a roasting tray. Put them in the oven for 15 minutes to dry out fully.

6   While the potatoes are in the oven, thinly slice the remaining onion. Heat the oil in a large, heavy-based frying pan and add the sliced onion and leeks. Fry over a medium heat for 10–15 minutes until soft and golden brown.

7   Add the potatoes to the pan and mix together, smashing the potato as you go. Fry for 5 minutes until the potatoes crisp up and start to turn golden brown. Next add the pulled ham hock and continue to fry for a further 3–5 minutes.

8   To make the hollandaise, place the egg yolks, lemon juice and salt into a heatproof bowl and set over a pan of simmering water (making sure the bottom of the bowl doesn't touch the water). Whisk for 20–30 seconds until the mixture thickens. It is important to keep the mixture moving at all times or the eggs will scramble.

9   Take the bowl off the pan of water, still whisking the mixture as you do so. Place the bowl onto a wet tea towel on your work surface (to ensure the bowl stays in position). Keep whisking the mixture all the while. Now add the melted butter in a thin stream, continuing to whisk until all the butter is absorbed. If the mixture becomes too thick at any stage, add a little bit of warm water, a tablespoon at a time, to thin it out. Set aside.

10   Remove the hash from the heat, stir through the parsley and mustard, and place the poached eggs on top of the dish. Place in the centre of the table with the hollandaise and peas to the side for guests to help themselves.

KIMCHI PANCAKE, SLOW-COOKED PORK BELLY AND FRIED DUCK EGGS

This is one of our favourite brunch dishes and it never fails to impress; it's a great combination of bold flavours and delicious textures. The added bonus is that the slow-cooked pork belly recipe can also be used as a lunch or dinner dish combined with seasonal leaves or vegetables. It pays to either get up super early to get the pork on or to prepare the pork the day before and simply reheat just before you serve it.

SERVES 4
1½ tbsp tahini
2 tbsp soy sauce
1 egg
120ml whole milk
1 tbsp rice wine vinegar
140g plain flour
1 tsp baking powder
250g Kimchi, roughly chopped
(see page 284 or use shop-bought)
3 spring onions, thinly sliced, plus extra
to garnish
Handful of roughly chopped coriander
leaves, plus extra to garnish
Vegetable oil, for frying
4 duck eggs or 8 hen eggs
Gochujang Ketchup (see page 280)
or sriracha sauce, to serve

SLOW-COOKED PORK BELLY
800g piece of boneless pork belly
Fine sea salt
1 litre Master Stock (see page 287)

1   Preheat the oven to 170°C and bring the master stock to the boil in a pan.

2   Place the pork in a high-sided roasting dish. Pour the hot master stock over the pork belly and cover with baking paper, then seal with foil. Place the pork in the oven and cook for 3½ hours or until the meat pulls apart easily.

3   Remove from the oven and carefully transfer the pork to a chopping board. Slice off the skin and pull the flesh apart with two forks. Put the shredded meat in a dish and spoon over several tablespoons of master stock from the roasting pan.

4   Increase the oven temperature to 180°C.

5   Whisk the tahini, soy sauce, egg, milk and vinegar together in a medium bowl. Sift the flour and baking powder into the bowl and stir until all is combined and you have a smooth batter. Add the kimchi, spring onions and coriander and stir together.

6   Heat a little oil in a heavy-based 20cm diameter skillet or oven-proof pan and pour half the batter in. Cook on one side for a few minutes, then place the pan in the oven for 10 minutes. Remove from the oven, flip the pancake over and return to the oven for a further 5 minutes. Repeat to make a second pancake.

7   While the pancakes are in the oven, fry the eggs to your liking.

8   To serve, cut each pancake into 8–12 pieces and arrange on plates with the hot slow-cooked pork and fried eggs. Garnish with coriander leaves and spring onion, and top with gochujang ketchup or sriracha sauce.

POACHING EGGS

The art of poaching eggs is simple as long as a few simple rules are followed. I get the best results in a deep saucepan rather than in a shallow one. The water should be properly boiling when the eggs go in but should not come back to the boil with the eggs in the water. This can make for damaged or broken eggs rather than amazing comet-shaped beauties.
I put vinegar in the water as it helps to set the egg faster and means the desired shape is achieved. If you don't like the flavour of the vinegar, don't use it – it is not essential. Below is a foolproof method for poaching the perfect egg. It is imperative that the eggs you are using are fresh and preferably free range and organic. (MK)

SERVES 4
2 litres water
80ml rice vinegar or white wine vinegar (do not use dark vinegars)
8 eggs

1   Bring the water to a rolling boil in a deep saucepan.

2   While you are waiting for the water to boil, crack the eggs into individual cups to ensure that none of the yolks are broken.

3   When the water is boiling add the vinegar, take a slotted spoon and start a whirlpool in the water. Stop stirring when the whirlpool has been created.

4   Drop the eggs one by one in quick succession into the middle of the water.

5   Once the last egg has gone in, set your timer for 3 minutes.

6   Do not let the water come back to a rolling boil with the eggs in the water.

7   When the time is up, remove your eggs with a slotted spoon and place the eggs on a clean tea towel to drain the excess water.

8   Serve immediately.

CORNBREAD

This is our version of the southern American classic and it has featured on our all-day menu – fried and served with chipotle butter, lime and fresh coriander – since our first day of trading. We now use it to make French toast for brunch (see page 70) and have turned it into a Latin American inspired breakfast dish for the restaurant with frijol negro salsa, fried eggs and hot sauce. It is the same basic bread recipe for all dishes and will remain a fixture on our menus as it is truly delicious. If you want to spice it up a bit, try adding some jalapeño chilli instead of the spring onions. It is delicious served warm with chipotle butter (see page 124) and will last in the fridge for up to 3 days.

MAKES 1 LOAF
60g butter, melted
3 eggs
400ml whole milk
170g instant polenta
80g strong white bread flour
1 tbsp caster sugar
1 tbsp baking powder
½ tsp fine sea salt
3 spring onions, thinly sliced
150g tinned sweetcorn kernels
(use fresh when in season)

1   Preheat the oven to 220°C and line a 23 × 13 × 7cm loaf tin with baking paper.

2   Pour the melted butter into a large bowl and add the eggs, whisking to combine, then whisk in the milk.

3   Sift the polenta, bread flour, caster sugar, baking powder and salt into a separate large bowl and mix to combine. Add the wet ingredients and mix carefully until there are no dry bits, being careful not to overwork the batter. Mix in the spring onions and sweetcorn kernels and stir to combine.

4   Pour into the prepared loaf tin and leave to rest for 10 minutes, then place in the oven. After 10 minutes reduce the oven temperature to 200°C and bake for a further 20–25 minutes, or until a skewer inserted into the centre comes out clean.

5   When the cornbread is ready, remove it from the oven and leave to cool in the tin for 5 minutes before turning out onto a wire rack.

INTRODUCTION

MORNING BREW

BREAKFAST

BRUNCH

LUNCH:

SOUPS & GRAINS,
SALADS, VEGETABLES

AFTERNOON TEA

DINNER

PUDDING

DRINKS

The menus at Caravan have always been consciously grain, salad and vegetable-focused. We direct our energies to locally grown, seasonal and lesser known varieties and often find our inspiration for dishes from what's on offer at our local farmers' market (the resurgence of these markets has meant that sourcing has never been easier). We also understand the part we play as a high-volume restaurant and the importance of giving people a delicious reason to choose something other than meat, the production of which can be a lot more environmentally intensive.

Our culinary approach to vegetables and salads is a 'less is more' philosophy: we believe that by applying a few simple, interesting, bold flavours to seasonal, locally grown vegetables or leaves you get the most honest and delicious results. The recipes in this chapter use global flavours, spices and herbs to enhance even the most basic leaf or grain. There are lots of recipes that are nourishing and wholesome, and a good measure of indulgent ones too. Most of our restaurant guests enjoy a combination of small plates as part of their dining experience, so we encourage you to play around with a number of different grain, vegetable or leaf dishes to create your own 'feast of plates' at home. Most importantly, cook with grains and vegetables as much as you can. They are good for you, better for the planet and taste so great, with minimal effort. Enough said.

PEARL BARLEY, LENTIL AND VEGETABLE SOUP WITH CRÈME FRAÎCHE AND SALSA VERDE

This soup is the kind that fills the whole kitchen with warmth and delicious smells. The liquid to grain ratio is pretty low, which means that after the first meal of soup you get from it, you will inevitably be left with a pot of barley and vegetables without enough liquid to call it a soup anymore. The leftover soup base is great served alongside a roast chicken with salsa verde.

SERVES 4–6

4 tbsp rapeseed oil or other neutral-flavoured oil
3 brown onions (about 500g), finely diced
3 carrots (about 250g), finely diced
3 celery sticks, finely diced
3 garlic cloves, chopped
2 bay leaves
4 thyme sprigs
100g Puy lentils
200g pearl barley
Sea salt and black pepper
Crème fraîche, to serve
Salsa Verde, to serve (see page 279)

1   Heat the oil in a large heavy-based pan, add the onions and carrots and cook over a medium heat for 5 minutes. Add the celery, garlic, bay and thyme cook for another 5 minutes.

2   Now add the lentils and barley and stir until the grains have been mixed evenly through vegetables. Cover with 2 litres of water, bring to the boil and boil for 5 minutes. Reduce the heat to a simmer and cook until the grains are tender, about 30–40 minutes. Season the soup with salt and pepper.

3   Portion into bowls and serve with a dollop each of crème fraîche and salsa verde on top.

BUTTERNUT SQUASH, COCONUT AND PICKLED GINGER SOUP

In the winter months, this is a wonderful warming soup, while in the summer it can be made in advance and served chilled. If you are serving it chilled, you may have to alter the consistency slightly with a little more coconut milk, as it will inevitably thicken during the cooling process.

SERVES 6

2 tbsp vegetable oil or coconut oil
3 shallots, halved and sliced
3 garlic cloves, crushed
2 small butternut squash (about 800g), peeled and diced
2 × 400ml tins coconut milk
Bunch of coriander (stalks and leaves)
40g Japanese pickled ginger
3 tbsp light soy sauce
1 tsp fine sea salt
2 tbsp lime juice
1 tbsp black sesame seeds, to garnish
2 tbsp coconut cream, to garnish

1   Heat the oil in a medium pan. Add the shallots and garlic and cook over a medium heat until the shallots soften, about 5 minutes.

2   Add the butternut squash, coconut milk and coriander stalks to the pan, along with 1 litre of cold water. Bring to the boil, then turn down the heat and simmer for 25 minutes until the butternut squash is soft.

3   Remove from the heat, add the ginger, soy sauce and salt and blend with a stick blender before passing the liquid through a fine sieve. Add the lime juice and serve garnished with the reserved coriander leaves, a sprinkle of black sesame seeds and a dollop of coconut cream.

RED QUINOA AND BUCKWHEAT GRAIN BOWL, SWEET POTATO, BROCCOLI, PEANUTS AND MISO-SESAME DRESSING

Full of slow-release energy goodness and packed with flavour, this Caravan classic now appears on all our menus. The quinoa forms the base of the salad, which is a great vehicle for any green or roasted root vegetable. You can substitute the sweet potato for baby carrots, parsnip or butternut squash and the broccoli can be swapped out for kale or Swiss chard. The dressing is delicious and will keep you going back for more.

SERVES 4
300g red quinoa, rinsed well
100ml Basic Soy Pickle (see page 277)
40g coriander leaves
300g sweet potato, peeled, diced into 3cm chunks and roasted
150g sprouting broccoli, blanched and refreshed in cold water
150ml Miso-sesame Dressing (see page 276)
60g peanuts, toasted
20g pumpkin seeds, toasted
20g toasted buckwheat (optional)

1   Place the quinoa in a large pan with double the volume of salted water and bring to the boil. Reduce the heat and simmer for 12 minutes. Drain away any excess water and leave to cool.

2   Place the red quinoa, soy pickle and half the coriander leaves in a bowl and give it a stir to distribute the coriander and coat the quinoa in soy pickle.

3   Add the roasted sweet potato chunks and the broccoli to the bowl and again stir to distribute the new additions.

4   Tip out onto a serving plate and evenly spread it out. Use a spoon to drizzle the miso-sesame dressing over the top of the salad. Finally, sprinkle over the peanuts, pumpkin seeds, buckwheat, if using, and the remaining coriander leaves.

QUINOA AND BUCKWHEAT GRAIN BOWL, CARROT AND SPINACH SLAW, AVOCADO, GREEK YOGHURT, HARISSA, SUPER SEEDS

I have been obsessed with grain bowls for a long time, and we have developed lots of delicious variations for both our brunch and all-day menus over the years. They are a great savoury and healthy way to kick-start the day and stay nourished throughout it. This grain bowl ticks three big boxes – it's full of healthy goodness, it looks great and most importantly it tastes amazing. (LHH)

SERVES 4

200g quinoa (we use a mixture of red and white), well rinsed
100g buckwheat groats, well rinsed
Small handful of flat-leaf parsley, finely chopped
½ tbsp finely chopped dill
½ tbsp finely chopped chives
4 tbsp Lemon Dressing (see page 108)
Handful of spinach leaves, thinly sliced
60g cucumber, thinly sliced
120g Greek yoghurt
4 tbsp Harissa (see page 278 or use shop-bought)
1 avocado, quartered
2 tbsp pumpkin seeds, toasted
2 tbsp sunflower seeds, toasted
2 soft boiled eggs, halved

PICKLED CARROT

400g carrots, cut into thin julienne strips
2 tsp caraway seeds, toasted
80ml apple cider vinegar
50ml water
60g caster sugar

1   Place the quinoa in a large pan with double the volume of salted water and bring to the boil. Reduce the heat and simmer for 12 minutes. Drain away any excess water and set aside to cool. Do the same with the buckwheat groats, simmering for just 10 minutes. Drain and set aside to cool.

2   To prepare the pickled carrot, place the julienne carrot and the caraway seeds into a large bowl. Place the vinegar, water and sugar in a small pan and bring to the boil. Pour the boiling liquid over the carrot and set aside to cool. Cover and store in the fridge.

3   Combine the cooked quinoa and buckwheat in a large bowl. Add the chopped herbs and lemon dressing and stir well to combine. Set aside.

4   Take 60g of the pickled carrot and add to a bowl, squeezing out any excess liquid. Add the sliced spinach and mix with your hands to form 'slaw'. The leftover pickled carrot will keep in the fridge for up to 2 weeks.

5   Divide the dressed grains between 4 serving bowls and pile it up so it forms an even platform to carry the rest of the ingredients. Place a quarter of the carrot slaw in a pile on each of the bowls and do the same with the sliced cucumber. Now evenly divide the yoghurt and the harissa between the 4 plates by way of a dollop of each on top of the grains.

6   Place an avocado quarter on each bowl with a soft boiled egg along side, then sprinkle with the toasted seeds. (Alternatively, layer all the ingredients in a large serving dish and place in the middle of the table for people to help themselves.)

BULGUR WHEAT WITH PRESERVED LEMON, SULTANAS, PINE NUTS, FETA, PARSLEY AND CORIANDER

This salad is excellent as a summer combo with barbecued meat or fish or by itself as a simple healthy lunch. The soused sultanas add a rich dimension to this recipe, so definitely make the effort to do these. You can prepare the bulgur wheat in advance as well, making it easy to pull the salad together when needed.

SERVES 4–6
225g coarse bulgur wheat
500ml water
50ml olive oil
½ tbsp fine sea salt
1 red onion, thinly sliced
85g pine nuts, toasted
200g feta cheese, crumbed
Handful of flat-leaf parsley, roughly chopped
Handful of coriander leaves, roughly chopped
1 tbsp cumin seeds, toasted
2 tbsp lemon juice
2 tbsp Preserved Lemon rind (see page 285 or use shop-bought), finely chopped
Sea salt and black pepper

SOUSED SULTANAS
225g sultanas
60ml balsamic vinegar
60ml red wine vinegar
120ml water
50g dark muscovado sugar

1 Place the bulgur wheat, water, olive oil and salt in a pan and bring to the boil. After 2 minutes, turn off the heat, cover with a lid and leave to steam for 20 minutes or until all the liquid is absorbed and the bulgur is soft and tender. Drain away any excess liquid and allow the bulgur to cool completely

2 Meanwhile put all the ingredients for the soused sultanas in a pan and bring to the boil. Simmer for 5 minutes and then remove from heat. (You can do this in advance as the sultanas will keep in the liquid for up to a week – just strain off the liquid before using.)

3 Combine the cooled bulgur with the soused sultanas and all the remaining ingredients in a large bowl and stir until evenly mixed. Taste and adjust the seasoning with salt and pepper. Transfer to a dish and serve.

CHICKPEAS, TOMATO, SORREL, FLATBREAD, BASIL YOGHURT, SUMAC

It is key to select tomatoes that are bursting with juice and flavour when making this salad, so it is best only to make this when amazing tomatoes are in season. The tomato mix resting time is also important as it allows the salt to extract the tomato juice, and flavour the olive oil with garlic and tomato essence. This juice becomes the dressing for the salad, and getting as much flavour into it is what will be the difference between a great salad and a mediocre one. In the restaurants, we chargrill flatbread to order and tear it into the salad. The best parts of this salad are the remaining pieces of bread that are completely soaked in the tomato, olive oil juice. They are little soggy treasures of deliciousness.

SERVES 4

250g dried chickpeas (or use
400g tinned)
500g vine plum tomatoes
1 tbsp fine sea salt, plus ¼ tsp
100ml olive oil
1 garlic clove, thinly sliced
5 basil sprigs
1 tsp bicarbonate of soda
4 tbsp Greek yoghurt
½ red onion, thinly sliced
2 pitta breads
50g sorrel leaves, roughly chopped,
(spinach is a good alternative)
2 tbsp sumac

1   Wash the chickpeas in cold running water, then place in a ceramic or glass bowl, cover with cold water and soak overnight. If using tinned chickpeas rinse them well under cold running water.

2   Cut each tomato into around 8 pieces, removing the core. Place in a medium bowl, add the tablespoon of sea salt the olive oil, garlic and 1 of the basil sprigs and massage the mixture with your hands. Cover with cling film or a clean tea towel and set aside at room temperature for at least 4 hours.

3   Drain the dried chickpeas and place them with the bicarbonate of soda into a medium pan and cover with water. Cook for 45 minutes–1 hour, until cooked through.

4   Place the ¼ teaspoon of sea salt and remaining basil stalks into a mortar and pestle and pound to a paste. Add the yoghurt to the mortar and stir through, then transfer to a small bowl and set aside.

5   When the chickpeas are cooked, drain, cool and add to the tomatoes with the sliced red onion.

6   Just before serving toast the pitta and break into pieces to mix through the salad. Transfer to a serving bowl, stir through the sorrel leaves and dollop over the basil yoghurt. Finally sprinkle over the sumac and serve.

SIMPLE SALADS, MANY WAYS

We love leaves of all shapes, colours and varieties. Rather than include a number of different green salad recipes, we elected to let you decide the green leaf combination and help you along with six simple, delicious dressings to go with them. As the name suggests, we like to keep our salads simple and so generally advise pairing 2–4 different leaf varieties together. Always try to choose leaves that will complement each other by way of texture, flavour and look. The combination of curly, leafy, frilly and stalky in different colours looks amazing on a plate with a simple dressing. To keep things really simple just dress with a splash of good-quality olive oil, a squeeze of lemon, pepper and salt or drizzle with good-quality, sweet balsamic vinegar; for some more inspiration, see the recipes on page 108.

Leaves that are particularly good in the autumn and winter months include mustard greens, winter purslane, mizuna, sorrel, radicchio, endive, frisée, escarole, kale and Arctic King lettuce.

In spring and summer go for cos, romaine, iceberg, baby gem, lollo rosso, all chards, spinach, rocket, watercress, wild nettles and dandelion greens.

For some added flavour, try some freshly torn herbs such as chervil, dill, parsley, mint, basil, tarragon or chives.

To bulk your salad out more, add some shaved fennel, radish, cucumber or courgette, or some plum or baby tomatoes, olives or avocado.

For a nice crunch, add some toasted pine nuts or pumpkin or sunflower seeds.

A good-quality shaved pecorino or Parmesan or some crumbly feta or goat's cheese will add a great extra dimension too.

DRESSINGS

50ml lemon juice
100ml olive oil
1 garlic clove, smashed
Sea salt and black pepper

LEMON

Combine the lemon juice and the olive oil in a jar with
a tight-fitting lid. Add the garlic clove and shake vigorously
with the lid on. Season to taste with salt and pepper. Store
in the fridge until needed (it will keep for up to 2 days) and
shake again before using.

5 Confit Garlic cloves (see page 276),
mashed with a fork
50ml sherry vinegar
100ml olive oil
1 tsp fresh thyme leaves
Sea salt and black pepper

CONFIT GARLIC, THYME AND SHERRY VINEGAR

Combine the confit garlic, vinegar, olive oil and thyme in
a bowl and whisk to combine. Season to taste with salt
and pepper. Store in an airtight container in the fridge for
up to a week.

80g Greek yoghurt
40ml filtered water
2 tbsp apple cider vinegar
50ml extra-virgin olive oil
½ garlic clove, smashed
1 tbsp finely chopped chives
¼ tsp fine sea salt
¼ tsp cracked black pepper

SIMPLE YOGHURT DRESSING

Combine the yoghurt, water, vinegar and oil in a bowl
and whisk together. Stir in the garlic, chives, salt and
pepper and allow to stand for at least half an hour to let
the flavours permeate the yoghurt. Use straight away
or store in an airtight container in the fridge for 3–4 days.

1 tbsp yuzu juice (you can find
this at most good supermarkets)
2 tbsp sake
80ml mirin
80ml sesame oil
30ml soy sauce

YUZU, SAKE AND MIRIN

Whisk all the ingredients together in a bowl or shake
together in a jar with a tight-fitting lid. This will
keep in an airtight container in the fridge for 2 weeks.

1 tbsp raw honey
1 tbsp English mustard
½ tbsp apple cider vinegar
½ tbsp filtered water
½ tsp fine sea salt
150ml rapeseed oil

APPLE CIDER VINEGAR, HONEY AND MUSTARD

In a bowl, whisk the honey, mustard, vinegar, water and
sea salt together until combined. Slowly add the oil as you
continuously whisk the contents of the bowl to emulsify
the ingredients. Store in an airtight container in the fridge
for up to a week.

25g umeboshi plums, pitted and
chopped (available from specialist
Japanese food shops)
10g honey (we use New
Zealand Manuka)
10ml red wine vinegar
15ml white truffle oil

TRUFFLED UMEBOSHI PLUM

Combine all the ingredients together in a bowl. This will
keep in an airtight container in the fridge for 2 weeks.

SPROUTING BROCCOLI, SWISS CHARD, BABY SPINACH, MEDJOOL DATES, PINE NUTS, RAS EL HANOUT

Full of flavour, colour, texture and freshness, this is a great salad to create for lunch or supper as purple sprouting broccoli arrives in season. You can use any type of broccoli here, but purple sprouting is particularly good.

SERVES 4
200g purple sprouting broccoli
1 tbsp ras el hanout
1 tbsp olive oil
Generous pinch of fine sea salt
1 tbsp rapeseed oil
80g Greek yoghurt
1 tbsp lemon juice
100g tender Swiss chard leaves, roughly torn
50g baby spinach leaves, roughly torn
100g pitted Medjool dates, torn in half
40g pine nuts, toasted

1   In a large bowl, toss the purple sprouting broccoli with half the ras el hanout, the olive oil and a generous pinch of sea salt. Heat a griddle pan (or a barbecue if the weather permits) and grill the broccoli until the edges go black and the broccoli is cooked. Transfer to a large serving bowl and allow to cool.

2   In a small frying pan, gently heat the rapeseed oil with the remaining ras el hanout. Cook the spices out over a low heat for around 3 minutes then scrape the oil into a small bowl and allow to cool before mixing into the Greek yoghurt with the lemon juice. Set aside.

3   Place the chard and the spinach leaves in the bowl with the broccoli, dollop on the flavoured yoghurt and gently toss so the broccoli and leaves are roughly coated with the dressing. Finally, sprinkle the dates and pine nuts over the top of the salad and serve.

BRUSSELS SPROUT AND RADISH SALAD, PRESERVED LEMON, GARLIC AND PANKO CRUMBS

We made this recently at a lunch for a huge group of friends and we were surprised that many of the group had never eaten raw Brussels sprouts before. With this recipe we wanted to celebrate the form of the Brussels sprouts as much as their great texture. So we have combined pulled round leaves with finely shaved inner leaves. The iced water will keep the Brussels sprouts really crisp as you are making the rest, but make sure you drain them really well before dressing. For this salad to sing, it is important to use Brussels at their best, when they are tightly packed and juicy. Controversially this could be a great alternative to Christmas dinner Brussels too.

SERVES 4–6
500g Brussels sprouts
4 tbsp crème fraîche
1 tbsp apple cider vinegar
3 tbsp olive oil
1 garlic clove, very finely chopped
30g panko breadcrumbs
Small handful of flat-leaf parsley, finely chopped
60g Preserved Lemon rind (see page 285 or use shop-bought), sliced
100g radishes, thinly sliced
Parmesan, to serve

1 Pull off two or three layers of the outer leaves of the Brussels sprouts (depending on their size), discarding any damaged or discoloured ones, and place in a large bowl of ice-cold water. Thinly shave the inner leaves of the Brussels sprouts using a mandolin or sharp knife and place in the bowl with the leaves.

2 In a small bowl mix together the crème fraîche and apple cider vinegar and set aside.

3 Heat the olive oil in a large frying pan and fry the minced garlic over a medium heat. Add the panko breadcrumbs and stir continuously until browned. Remove from the heat and once the breadcrumbs are cool, stir through the chopped parsley.

4 Drain the Brussels sprouts thoroughly and then place into a large bowl. Stir in the preserved lemon rind and sliced radishes and then turn out on to a serving dish. Pour over the crème fraîche and vinegar mixture and top with the breadcrumbs and parsley. Scatter with some freshly grated Parmesan to serve.

CHOPPED KALE SALAD, LEMON BAKED RICOTTA, SHAVED FENNEL, PINE NUTS, PECORINO

Kale, much like avocado, is one of those healthy, full-of-goodness vegetables that has found its way onto many a restaurant menu in recent years. We genuinely love it at Caravan, in spite of the hype, and use it on our pizzas, in our drinks and in this salad. You can use curly kale or Tuscan kale, otherwise known as cavolo nero. We have recently started using baby kale grown specifically for us by GrowUp Urban Farms, an inner-city, sustainable, indoor growing facility in east London. Whether you use curly or Tuscan, make sure you use the tender smaller leaves; if you can't find these, blanch the kale in boiling water for 90 seconds, and refresh in cold water. If you love kale like we do, you will love this salad.

SERVES 4
180g ricotta
Zest of 1 unwaxed lemon
25ml olive oil
Sea salt and black pepper
200g tender kale leaves, stems removed
75ml Lemon Dressing (see page 108)
½ bulb fennel, shaved
75g pine nuts, toasted
30g pecorino, shaved

1   Preheat the oven to 180°C.

2   Put the ricotta in a small ovenproof baking dish. Sprinkle over the lemon zest, olive oil and a pinch of sea salt and cracked black pepper over the top of the ricotta. Use the back of a spoon to push down on the ricotta, breaking it apart into pieces. Place the dish in the oven and bake for 20 minutes, then remove from the oven and allow to cool.

3   Meanwhile roughly chop the kale leaves and place into a large serving bowl. Note: if you are using later season, tougher kale or curly kale, you will need to blanch it in boiling water for 90 seconds, refresh in cold water and spin in a salad spinner to remove the excess moisture. Ten minutes before serving, dress the kale with the lemon dressing and mix well – you need to almost massage the dressing into the leaves. This will soften any tough leaves.

4   Just before serving, toss the shaved fennel through the greens, then crumble over the baked ricotta. Scatter the pine nuts on top and gently fold to mix everything together. Finally, shave the pecorino over the top of the salad.

KIMCHI SLAW

Kimchi slaw is one of those winning combinations, bringing an often-needed salad kick to your summer barbecue. Great with baby back ribs, chargrilled lamb cutlets, courgette and aubergine or with any barbecue when you just want to be a bit more adventurous with the flavours. The diffused kimchi flavour works really well, especially with fatty ribs where the cabbage brings a refreshing crunch to the party.

SERVES 6
250g Kimchi (see page 284 or use shop-bought)
250g red cabbage, thinly sliced
80g Mayonnaise (see page 273 or use shop-bought)
2 tsp fine sea salt
Handful of coriander leaves, roughly chopped

1   Combine the kimchi, red cabbage, mayonnaise and sea salt in a medium bowl and stir to combine.

2   Add the coriander leaves and give it another light stir before serving. Serve.

SOBA NOODLES, SHIMEJI MUSHROOMS, PICKLED GINGER, SHISO, SESAME-SOY DRESSING

Inspired by our travels, this bowl of cold, full-flavoured noodles will transport you to Japan. The simple, clean flavours that the Japanese do so well work perfectly in harmony with one another and make for a refreshing, healthy, light noodle salad. Shimeji mushrooms are native to East Asia, but are also grown commercially in northern Europe, so you should be able to find these at specialist grocers, good supermarkets and Asian supermarkets. Feel free to experiment with other Asian mushrooms, such as shiitake.

SERVES 4
200g soba noodles
60ml light soy sauce
60ml rice wine vinegar
60ml mirin
40g Japanese pickled ginger purée
10ml sesame oil
2 tbsp rapeseed oil
150g shimeji mushrooms (or use shiitake)
3 spring onions, finely chopped
Small handful of coriander leaves
1 tsp sesame seeds
Few shiso or basil leaves (optional)

1   Bring a litre of water to the boil. Place the soba noodles into the boiling water and stir the noodles so they do not stick; cook for around 3 minutes until just beyond al dente. Drain and then cool the noodles in a bowl of cold water to stop them cooking further. Once fully cool, drain and set aside.

2   In a small bowl, combine the soy sauce, vinegar, mirin, pickled ginger and sesame oil. Pour a quarter of this mixture into another small bowl and set aside.

3   Heat the rapeseed oil in a medium frying pan, then add the shimeji mushrooms and sauté over a high heat until nicely browned. Remove from the heat and deglaze the pan with the reserved smaller amount of dressing. Allow the mushrooms to cool.

4   Combine the noodles in a large bowl with the mushrooms and dressing. Add the spring onions and the coriander and gently toss the salad to mix everything together.

5   Tip the noodle salad into a serving bowl and top with the sesame seeds and the shiso or basil leaves, if using. Serve.

BURMESE CHICKEN SALAD, TURMERIC, CHILLI, LIME, PEANUTS

The origins of this salad come from Burma, via a restaurant in Christchurch, New Zealand, called the Bohdi Tree. Our head chef at Caravan Exmouth Market, Nick Anderson, used to talk about this salad as one of the best things ever. We asked him to come up with a version and this is what happened. It has been on and off our menus for years with slight alterations each time, but this is our favourite version. If you have trouble finding green papaya or kohlrabi, you can replace these ingredients with cucumber, celery, thinly sliced cabbage or unripe or green mango.

SERVES 4–6
4 skinless chicken breasts, ideally free-range
1 tbsp nam pla (fish sauce)
40g fresh ginger, peeled and finely sliced
4 coriander stalks
2 large carrots, peeled and julienned
60g spinach leaves, sliced
½ green papaya, julienned
150g kohlrabi, julienned
1 red chilli, sliced
Handful of coriander leaves, roughly chopped
Handful of mint leaves, roughly chopped
100g peanuts, toasted and crushed

THE DRESSING
200ml vegetable oil or other neutral-flavoured oil
1 large brown onion, thinly sliced
2 garlic cloves, thinly sliced
20g fresh ginger, peeled and finely chopped
1 tsp ground turmeric
1 tsp hot smoked paprika
Zest of 3 limes
150ml lime juice
80ml nam pla (fish sauce)

1 First poach the chicken. Place the chicken breasts in a single layer into a pan – ideally the breasts should fit quite snugly on the bottom of the pan. Pour over 750ml water, or enough to just cover the breasts. Add the fish sauce, ginger and coriander stalks.

2 Place over a high heat to bring the liquid to the boil quickly, then reduce the heat to as gentle a simmer as your stove allows. Cover with a lid and allow to simmer gently for 8 minutes. Turn the heat off and set aside with the lid on for a further 20 minutes. Remove the chicken from the liquid and set aside to cool. Once cool, shred the chicken, making sure to tear the breasts lengthways to ensure long strips of meat. Set aside.

3 To make the dressing, heat a little of the vegetable oil in a pan over a medium heat and gently sweat the onions, garlic and ginger for 5–10 minutes until everything has completely softened but not browned.

4 Add the remainder of the oil to the pan with the turmeric and paprika and simmer for a few minutes so that the spices lose their 'raw' taste. Transfer the contents of the pan to a bowl and allow to cool completely. When completely cooled, add the lime zest and juice and fish sauce to the bowl and mix to combine. Taste and adjust with more lime juice or fish sauce as you see fit. Store the dressing in the fridge until ready to use – it will keep in an airtight container in the fridge for up to 5 days.

5 To assemble the salad, mix the shredded chicken in a large bowl with the carrot, spinach, green papaya and kohlrabi. Add the dressing, chilli and herbs and mix well. Transfer the salad to a serving dish and sprinkle crushed peanuts over the top to serve.

NOTE

We use a mandolin to prepare our julienned vegetables so that we get super-long spaghetti-style strips. If you don't have a mandolin, use a vegetable peeler to create long strips, which you can fold in half, end on end, and then finely slice with a sharp knife.

SMASHED CUCUMBERS, SICHUAN CHILLI OIL, SESAME-SOY DRESSING

New Zealand has a thriving Chinese community. Many of the first travellers arrived in the country in the 1860s during the gold rush that occurred in the south of the country. These early settlers stayed and have subsequently enriched New Zealand's history, both culturally and culinarily – Chinese flavours and cooking styles have influenced our lives from an early age and so made their way onto our menus.

This dish is an excellent intro to a meal or can happily sit alongside a piece of steamed fish and wok-fried greens. It is earthy, salty, sweet, hot and refreshingly cooling all at once.

SERVES 6 AS A SNACK
OR SIDE DISH
6 small baby cucumbers
1 tbsp fine sea salt
180ml Basic Soy Pickle (see page 277)
4 tbsp Sichuan Chilli Oil (see page 281)
Black sesame seeds, to serve
Small handful of chopped coriander, to serve
Flaky sea salt, to serve
2 spring onions, finely chopped (optional)

SESAME-SOY DRESSING
60g tahini
30ml water
1 tsp lemon juice
½ tsp light soy sauce
½ small garlic clove, minced

1   Cut the cucumbers in half lengthways and then again into thick slices. Use the palm of your hand or the back of a knife to gently smash them. Place the cucumbers in a bowl and sprinkle the fine sea salt over them. Mix through and set aside for 20 minutes.

2   Pour the cucumbers into a colander or sieve to drain off any excess moisture and then rinse off the salt under cold running water. Return the cucumbers to the bowl, pour over the basic soy pickle and set aside. This should be done the day before, or at least 3 hours ahead.

3   In a small bowl whisk together all the ingredients for the sesame soy dressing and set aside.

4   When you are ready to serve, remove the cucumbers from the soy pickle and strain thoroughly.

5   Combine the cucumbers and sesame soy dressing in a medium bowl, mixing to ensure the cucumbers are covered. Transfer to a small serving bowl and spoon over the Sichuan chilli oil, making sure you get some of the chilli flakes in as well. Sprinkle with black sesame seeds, coriander leaves, sea salt and the spring onions, if using, and serve.

FRIED CORNBREAD, CHIPOTLE BUTTER, CORIANDER, SPRING ONIONS, LIME

This cornbread recipe has been a hugely popular staple on our menu since we first opened in Exmouth Market in 2010. We make so much of it that the chefs can do it with their eyes closed. It is perfect served in the middle of the table with any course and acts as a great substitute to sliced bread. We also love it as a pre-dinner snack with a cold brew. Here we have served it with Chipotle Butter which is totally delicious.

MAKES 10 SLICES
1 Cornbread loaf (see page 87)
2 tbsp olive oil, for frying
Coriander leaves
2 spring onions, sliced
2 limes, cut into wedges

CHIPOTLE BUTTER
125g unsalted butter, softened
½ tsp chipotle chillies, very
finely chopped
Zest and juice of ½ lime
¼ tsp sea salt
Small handful of coriander
(leaves and tender stalks), chopped

1   Place all the chipotle butter ingredients in a bowl and beat to combine and distribute all the ingredients evenly through the butter. Chill the butter in the fridge until needed (it can be stored there for 2 weeks, in an airtight cotainer).

2   Trim the ends of the cornbread loaf and cut into 10 equal slices.

3   Working in batches, heat a little olive oil in a pan over a medium heat and pan-fry the sliced cornbread on both sides until golden brown.

4   Serve straight away with the sliced chipotle butter, coriander leaves, spring onions and lime wedges.

SHELLING PEAS, BROAD BEANS, MINT AND RICOTTA

Christmas in New Zealand is the time of year for shelling peas and broad beans. When we were kids it was always our job before big lunches to sit down together and remove the peas and beans from their pods, and we have extremely fond memories of those times. We used to think we were being a real help to the proceedings; that without us, it would not have been possible to get the lunch ready in time. We were pea-shelling champions and the race was on. Now, with children of our own, we see the very needed distraction that this seemingly important job created and we encourage our kids to help with such tasks ourselves. It is also such a great way to get kids engaged in food and as a result they enjoy eating it more. Everybody is a winner in the preparation of shelling peas and broad beans it would seem! We have created this dish with ricotta, but it would also go very well with burrata.

SERVES 4
300g ricotta
1 tsp fine sea salt
1 tsp cracked black pepper
Juice of 1 lemon
200g frozen or freshly shelled peas
300g frozen or freshly podded
broad beans
1 green chilli, sliced
2 spring onions, sliced
Few mint leaves
Small handful of flat-leaf
parsley leaves
80ml olive oil

1   Combine the ricotta, sea salt, pepper and lemon juice in a bowl and set aside.

2   Bring a large pan of salted water to the boil and drop in the peas and broad beans. Cook for around 3 minutes at a rolling boil, then drain and refresh in cold water. Drain thoroughly and tip into a large bowl.

3   Add the chilli, spring onions, mint, parsley and olive oil and toss together.

4   Smear the ricotta directly onto a serving plate (or individual plates). Spoon the dressed peas and broad beans over the ricotta and serve.

ASPARAGUS, SWEET MISO, BLUE CHEESE, HERBS

Asparagus is one of those vegetables in the seasonal calendar that we all eagerly anticipate in the UK. As soon as the harvesting starts, traditionally on St George's day, the restaurant world goes into overdrive and you will find asparagus on any self-respecting restaurant menu for the duration of the short season. Miso and blue cheese might not seem like the obvious pairing with asparagus, but the sweetness of the miso, coupled with the saltiness of the cheese and fresh Asian herbs, really works. Grilling the asparagus on the barbecue or a griddle also works really well with this dish and adds a charred, smoky dimension to the flavours.

Den miso is something that you can't live without once you've made it. We use it to marinate fish before grilling or baking, and it is also delicious on grilled aubergines. When mixed with a little English mustard, it also makes a great marinade for barbecued steaks.

SERVES 4
12 asparagus spears, stem-ends snapped off
Small handful of Thai basil leaves, roughly torn (or use regular basil)
75g Stilton
2 tbsp shiso cress (optional)
1 tsp white sesame seeds, toasted

DEN MISO
80ml sake
80ml mirin
200g white miso paste
350g unrefined caster sugar

1   First make the den miso. Pour the sake and mirin into a medium pan and bring to the boil to cook off the alcohol. Add the miso paste and whisk together over a medium heat. Bring the contents of the pan back to the boil and add a quarter of the sugar. Continue to whisk until the sugar is dissolved. Repeat with half the remaining sugar; once dissolved, add the last of the sugar and whisk to dissolve.

2   Cook for 5 minutes over a medium heat or until the mixture boils. Set the pan aside and allow the sauce to cool. This will make about 450–500ml but the leftover den miso can be stored in an airtight container in the fridge for up to 3 weeks.

3   Bring a large pan of well-salted water to the boil. Drop in the asparagus spears and cook for 3 minutes, then drain and refresh in cold water. Transfer to a medium bowl.

4   Add 4 tablespoons of the den miso and the basil and mix well to make sure the asparagus is covered in the sauce. Arrange the dressed asparagus on a serving plate in a nice even layer. Crumble the Stilton evenly over the top and sprinkle with the shiso cress, if using, and sesame seeds. Serve.

CHARRED BABY LEEKS WITH CONFIT GARLIC BUTTER

Baby leeks or calçots (Catalonian spring onions) are perfect for this recipe, but if you are unable to find either don't be put off – larger leeks will also yield great results, just up the cooking time in the oven a bit; depending on size, you may also want to slice the leeks into halves or thirds. Wherever possible we love charring over coals for the honest, smoky flavours, but of course a griddle pan will also work. If you are charring the leeks over coals, toss them with a mixture of water and olive oil before placing on the grill. The water will produce steam and allow a more even cooking at the outset.

SERVES 4
100g Confit Garlic (see page 276)
150g unsalted butter, softened
Handful of flat-leaf parsley leaves,
finely chopped
1 tsp fine sea salt
4 tbsp rapeseed oil
10 baby leeks
Chopped parsley and thyme leaves,
to garnish
Chilli flakes, to garnish

1   Preheat the oven to 180°C.

2   Place the confit garlic, butter, parsley and salt in a small bowl and mix together. Set aside.

3   Heat the oil in a large griddle pan and char the leeks over a high heat until charred on all sides. Reduce the heat and continue to cook for a further 4–5 minutes until the leeks are soft throughout.

4   Arrange the leeks on a serving plate and top with the garlic confit butter. Serve straight away as the butter melts with some freshly chopped parsley, thyme leaves and chilli flakes.

ROASTED, PICKLED AND RAW BEETS WITH CHÈVRE

This dish started life as a lead dish for a summer feasting session we did many years back called 'Smoked, Pickled and Raw'. To make this easier to prepare at home, we have changed the smoked element to a roasted beet instead of a smoked beet purée. It is all about the combination of textures that makes this dish work. You can use something other that goat's cheese if you like but it needs a really good strong-tasting white cheese to enhance the flavour and contrast the colours.

SERVES 4
100g small striped pink beetroot
150g goat's cheese, crumbled
(or use goat's curd)
Few mint leaves, torn
or roughly chopped
1 tbsp olive oil
Sea salt and black pepper

ROASTED RED BEETS
500g baby red beetroot, unpeeled
and with stems trimmed to 3cm
25ml red wine vinegar
50ml olive oil
½ tsp fine sea salt
½ tsp cracked black pepper

PICKLED GOLDEN BEETS
250g baby golden beetroot, peeled,
quartered and with stems trimmed
to 3cm
300ml apple cider vinegar
50g caster sugar

1   Preheat the oven to 170°C.

2   Wrap the whole, unpeeled baby red beetroot in a foil parcel with the vinegar, oil, salt and pepper. Carefully place the parcel in the oven and roast until the beetroot are soft in the middle, around 25 minutes, or until easily pierced with a knife.

3   Remove the cooked beetroot from the oven and allow it to cool, then chop each one into quarters. Transfer the beetroot quarters and any juices from the foil parcel to a bowl and set aside while you prepare the pickled golden beetroot.

4   Combine the quartered baby golden beetroot, vinegar, sugar and 800ml water in a pan. Bring the pan to the boil, then turn down to a simmer and cook for approximately 45 minutes until the beetroot is soft. Turn off the heat, set aside and allow the beetroot to cool in the liquid.

5   Slice the striped pink beetroot as thinly as you can (use a mandolin if you have one) and place them straight into a bowl of ice-cold water.

6   To assemble the dish, arrange the roasted red beetroot on a serving dish, draining off any juices as you lift them out of the bowl. Add the pickled golden beetroot. Place the goat's cheese in any gaps or straight on top of the beetroot, making sure not to cover the beaut-iful colours in a veil of white cheese. Complete the dish with the sliced pink beets and torn mint leaves – insert some of the sliced beetroot nearly vertically into any gaps between the beets to give the dish some visual texture.

7   Drizzle the plate with some good olive oil, sprinkle with salt and pepper and serve. You can also use some of the red liquid from roasting.

PICKLED SHIMEJI MUSHROOMS WITH EDAMAME-TOFU PURÉE

Whilst the two elements of this recipe are delicious when paired with each other, both also stand up in their own right as well. The pickled mushrooms and their accompanying drizzle make a great garnish for a piece of white fish or chicken and they are also lovely tossed through a salad of leaves, avocado and seeds, for example, or with some cold soba noodles as on page 118. These days it is relatively easy to buy frozen edamame beans. The edamame purée makes an excellent alternative to a hummus-style dip and can be served with toasted flatbread and/or raw vegetables. The combination of the two, however, is a creamy, pickled symphony.

SERVES 4
PICKLED MUSHROOMS
200g shimeji mushrooms
(or use shiitake)
2 tbsp vegetable oil
200g Basic Soy Pickle (see
page 277)
40ml olive oil
40ml white truffle oil
2 tbsp roughly chopped coriander
1 spring onion, thinly sliced
1 tbsp toasted buckwheat (optional)
Shiso cress or basil leaves (optional)

EDAMAME-TOFU PURÉE
300g edamame beans, podded
200g firm silken tofu
2 tbsp olive oil
3 tbsp lemon juice
½ tbsp fine sea salt
½ tsp cracked pepper

1   Heat the vegetable oil in a medium frying pan and fry the mushrooms over a medium heat until browned all over.

2   Combine the soy pickle and olive and truffle oils in a medium bowl, pour in the cooked mushrooms and stir to combine. Leave to cool before adding the chopped coriander and spring onion. Set aside while you make the edamame-tofu purée.

3   Bring a pan of water to the boil and blanch the edamame beans for 2 minutes; drain and refresh under cold water. When cooled, place in a food processor with the tofu and pulse to a rough consistency. Add the remaining ingredients and pulse to combine.

4   To serve, spread the purée over the base of a large serving plate (or individual plates) and spoon the mushrooms over the top. This is great with some toasted buckwheat sprinkled over the top, and a few shiso cress or basil leaves.

CHARRED SWEETCORN, GOAT'S BUTTER, PECORINO, CHILLI, LIME

We seem to always have leftovers of this pecorino seasoning mixture in a small plastic container in our fridge. I can't resist eating little pinches of it because it is so delicious. My partner, Renée, came up with the idea of adding cumin seeds to the seasoning mixture, which we feel totally makes this dish. You can make the mixture a day or two in advance and let the flavours develop. It is great for people trying to avoid dairy products (from cows).

The corn is a great side for a barbecue lunch or dinner, and is excellent with Chargrilled Lamb Cutlets with Chermoula (see page 208). If the weather does not permit barbecuing, use a griddle pan. Just make sure you get the corn nicely charred at the edges. (MK)

SERVES 4

4 corn cobs, husks removed (if cooking on a barbecue, peel the husks back and leave them attached and omit the par-boiling stage)
1 tbsp cumin seeds, toasted and crushed in a mortar and pestle
½ tbsp flaked sea salt
100g pecorino, grated (or use Parmesan)
½ tsp chilli flakes
Large handful of coriander (stalks and leaves), finely chopped
Zest of 2 unwaxed lemons
Zest of 2 limes
60g goat's butter, melted (or use cow's butter)
Coriander leaves, to garnish
Lime wedges, to serve

1   Preheat the oven to 200°C. Place a heavy-based roasting dish in the oven for 10–15 minutes to heat up.

2   In the meantime, place in a large pan of salted boiling water. Cook for 4–5 minutes until cooked, then drain and set aside to cool.

3   Mix the cumin seeds, salt, pecorino, chilli and coriander together in a bowl.

4   Carefully remove the roasting dish from the oven and scatter the lemon and lime zest directly onto the base of the dish and allow it to stand for 5 minutes. This will dry out the zest. Once dry, combine the zest with the ingredients in the mixing bowl.

5   Barbecue or griddle the corn over a medium-high heat until nice and coloured on all sides, then tip into a bowl and pour over the melted butter.

6   Tip onto a serving dish, sprinkle the seasoning over the top and scatter with coriander leaves. Serve with lime wedges and enjoy with a cold beer.

SPICED ROASTED CAULIFLOWER, HARISSA, POMEGRANATE YOGHURT

Roasting is our favourite way to cook this amazingly versatile vegetable. It looks beautiful on a plate with the edges a little charred and crispy. Cauliflower is also a brilliant vehicle for flavour and here the spiced oil infiltrates every nook and cranny of the heads and releases a juicy punch of flavour when you bite into it. The harissa and pomegranate yoghurt give the dish that extra hit of flavour and makes for lovely presentation too.

SERVES 4
1 large cauliflower
4 tbsp rapeseed oil or other neutral-flavoured oil
1 tbsp olive oil
25g Garam Masala (see page 286 or use shop-bought)
75g Greek yoghurt
15g pomegranate molasses
100g Harissa (see page 278) or use shop-bought)
1 tbsp nigella seeds
2 tbsp pomegranate seeds
Sea salt
Nigella seeds, to garnish

1   Preheat the oven to 180°C.

2   Cut the cauliflower into quarters and then cut each quarter in half, so you have 8 wedges of cauliflower.

3   Heat the rapeseed oil in a large frying pan and fry 4 pieces of cauliflower on each side until golden brown. Remove from the pan and repeat with the remaining 4 pieces. Place the cauliflower into a large bowl, pour in the olive oil and garam masala and toss to ensure a good coating on all sides, then tip the cauliflower onto a large roasting tray and place in the oven for 8–10 minutes.

4   Meanwhile combine the Greek yoghurt with the pomegranate molasses in a small bowl and season with salt; set aside.

5   Spread a tablespoon of harissa over the base of each serving plate, then place a couple of wedges of cauliflower on top of that. Dollop on spoonfuls of pomegranate molasses yoghurt and sprinkle with nigella seeds and pomegranate seeds. Finally, sprinkle with nigella seeds and serve.

ROASTED JERUSALEM ARTICHOKES, GIROLLES

The combination of crisp roasted artichokes with the soft girolles is texture heaven, and both ingredients bring an earthy deliciousness to the plate. Jerusalem artichokes can be unforgiving if undercooked so don't be afraid to cook them until they are really crisp on the outside and soft in the middle. The girolles would be absolutely delicious on a piece of sourdough toast in the morning for breakfast or with Braised Rabbit (see page 216) or Slow-cooked Lamb (see page 220). If you love truffle oil, add a few small drops at the end to enhance the flavours even more.

SERVES 4
800g Jerusalem artichokes, scrubbed thoroughly and cut into 2cm chunks
5 tbsp olive oil
20g unsalted butter
8 thyme sprigs
1 garlic clove, finely sliced
200g girolles
Small handful of flat-leaf parsley, finely chopped
Juice of ½ lemon
Sea salt and black pepper
Few drops of truffle oil, to finish (optional)

1   Preheat the oven to 200°C.

2   Put the artichoke chunks in a large bowl, add 4 tablespoons of the olive oil and season generously with salt, pepper and thyme. Toss through so that they are all totally coated in oil and seasoning.

3   Arrange the artichokes on a roasting tray in a single layer and place in oven for 40–45 minutes until soft and caramelised. They will need a stir/shake now and then to ensure they are browned all over. Remove from the oven and set aside.

4   Heat the remaining tablespoon of oil and the butter in a large frying pan and add the sliced garlic. Cook over a low heat for a minute, then turn up the heat and add the girolles. Fry over a high heat until browned, about 3–4 minutes.

5   Reduce the heat and then throw in the chopped parsley and lemon juice and season with salt and pepper.

6   Scatter the cooked girolles on top of the artichokes, spoon over all the excess butter and parsley and serve immediately, drizzled with a few drops of truffle oil, if using.

ROASTED AUBERGINE, CITRUS, RED ONION

This intensely flavoured, chunky relish of sorts is a great accompaniment to lamb but would work well with chargrilled fish or vegetable as well. It is important to get the aubergine really brown and caramelised in the pan to bring out the sweet, smoky flavours and ensure they are soft.

SERVES 4–6

3 medium aubergines (about 750g), cut into 3cm chunks
150ml rapeseed oil
1 medium red onion, thinly sliced into rings
Zest of 2 unwaxed lemons
50ml lemon juice
60ml olive oil
1 tbsp cumin seeds
½ tbsp fennel seeds
2 tsp fine sea salt
1 tsp black pepper, freshly ground
Handful of flat-leaf parsley, roughly chopped

1   Preheat the oven to 180°C.

2   Place the diced aubergine in a large bowl and toss with 50ml of the rapeseed oil. Heat another 50ml of rapeseed oil in a large frying pan and fry half the aubergine until brown on all sides. Remove from the pan and set aside. Add the remaining oil and fry the second batch of aubergines – don't be afraid to add more oil during the frying process if required. (Alternatively, if you have a deep fryer you can deep-fry the diced aubergines in there. It is really important they are completely fried and brown all over.)

3   When all the aubergine chunks are browned, put them into a roasting tray and roast in the oven for 15–20 minutes until soft.

4   In a large mixing bowl, combine the sliced onion, lemon zest and juice and set aside.

5   Heat the olive oil in a pan, add the cumin and fennel seeds and gently heat until the seeds start to colour. Turn off the heat and allow to cool before pouring over the onions.

6   Add the roasted aubergine, salt, pepper and parsley to the bowl and mix to combine before serving.

ROASTED BUTTERNUT SQUASH, BUTTERMILK DRESSING, TAMARI PUMPKIN SEEDS, DILL

You can use any type of squash or pumpkin for this dish and in fact using two different types if that is what you have to hand will add to the flavours and colour dimensions of the dish. Try to find butternuts or pumpkins of the same size so you have a rustic uniformity to the pieces. To spice this dish up, you can sprinkle on chilli flakes or shichimi togarashi, a Japanese 7-spice mixture with chilli. We make our own (see page 285) but you can source it from most Asian supermarkets.

SERVES 4–6
800g butternut squash
2 tbsp extra-virgin olive oil
20g pumpkin seeds
30ml soy sauce (we use gluten-free tamari)
2 tbsp chopped dill
Sea salt and black pepper

BUTTERMILK DRESSING
80ml buttermilk
30g Mayonnaise (see page 273 or use shop-bought)
2 Confit Garlic cloves (see page 276)
10ml white wine vinegar
10 chives, finely chopped

1 Preheat the oven to 180°C.

2 Peel the squash and cut into quarters lengthways, then cut in half again. Remove the seeds, ensuring no stringy parts are left.

3 Put the squash pieces in a large bowl, add the olive oil and season with salt and pepper. Give the bowl a good shake to coat the squash with oil and to evenly distribute the salt and pepper. Tip the seasoned squash onto a roasting tray and place into the oven for around 15–20 minutes, or until just soft all the way through. Remove from the oven and set aside to cool.

4 Mix the pumpkin seeds and soy sauce together in a bowl and give them a toss to make sure all the seeds are evenly coated. Pour the contents of the bowl onto a roasting tray, in a single layer, and place in the oven for 6–10 minutes. Remove the tray from the oven every few minutes and stir. You will know when they are done when all the tamari has evaporated. Remove from the oven and set aside to cool. (These will keep for a couple of days but are much better when used straight away.)

5 Meanwhile, make the buttermilk dressing. Place all the ingredients in a bowl and whisk together until smooth and fully combined. Set aside until needed – this will keep in the fridge for 2–3 days.

6 To assemble the dish, scatter the squash over a serving plate. Drizzle the buttermilk dressing over the top of the squash and sprinkle with the chopped dill and tamari pumpkin seeds.

CORIANDER FALAFEL, GREEN CHILLI ZHOUG, TAHINI, GREEK YOGHURT

Falafel has made regular appearances on our menus over the years. They make a great companion to a glass of wine at the bar or as part of a feast of small plates that is the backbone of our dining philosophy at the restaurants. We have served it alone as a small plate and as a component of a mezze plate with pickles, charcuterie and other treats. At home we also love eating it rolled up in flatbread with leftover slow-roasted lamb shoulder. However you serve it, this version will definitely add full-on flavour to your feast.

SERVES 4
400g dried chickpeas, soaked overnight in cold water
1½ tsp black peppercorns
1 tbsp cumin seeds
1 tbsp coriander seeds
1 small red onion, chopped
3 garlic cloves, chopped
50g coriander, leaves and stalks
40g flat-leaf parsley, leaves and stalks
1 tsp red chilli flakes
1 tsp flaked sea salt
180ml rapeseed oil
4 tbsp Green Chilli Zhoug
(see page 279)

TAHINI YOGHURT
300g Greek yoghurt
75g tahini
1½ tsp fine sea salt
1½ tsp lemon juice

1   Preheat the oven to 170°C and rinse and drain the soaked chickpeas.

2   Place all the ingredients for the tahini yoghurt in a small mixing bowl and stir together. Chill in the fridge until ready to serve.

3   Dry-roast the black peppercorns, cumin and coriander seeds in a frying pan over a medium heat until aromatic. Use a spice grinder or mortar and pestle to grind to a powder and set aside.

4   Put the onion, garlic, coriander, parsley, chilli flakes and salt into a food processor and blend to a paste. Add the soaked chickpeas and toasted spices and blend to a coarse texture.

5   Take a bit of the mixture out and squeeze it in your hand; it should hold its shape and release some moisture when squeezed firmly. Mould the mixture into 15–20 patties, using roughly 2 tablespoons per serving.

6   Heat the rapeseed oil in a frying pan – you want the oil to be around 1cm deep in the pan. Fry the falafel in batches until browned on both sides. Transfer to a baking tray while you cook the rest of the falafel. When all the falafel have been fried, place the baking tray into the oven and cook for a further 10 minutes. (Alternatively, if you have a deep fryer you won't need the oven. Heat the oil to 170°C and fry the falafel in batches for 4–5 minutes.)

7   Serve with the tahini yoghurt and green chilli zhoug.

BLUE CHEESE AND PEANUT WONTONS

These are famous in Wellington, if not the whole of New Zealand. Their precise origin is unclear: it was either of two fantastic restaurants, Café Paradiso or Castro's. Our version has been on the menu at Caravan since day one and is there to stay. We've included the recipe here as they are fantastic with a drink. They are an unexpected and delicious symphony of tangy, nutty and crunchy, and they are perfect with a beer.

MAKES 25 WONTONS
100g Stilton or other strong
blue cheese
100g crunchy peanut butter
10g coriander, finely chopped
1 green chilli, deseeded and
finely chopped
½ garlic clove, grated
1 tsp very finely chopped ginger
1 spring onion, thinly sliced
30g peanuts, toasted and chopped
25 wonton wrappers
Vegetable oil, for frying
Sticky Soy (see page 280), to serve

1   Place the Stilton, peanut butter, coriander, green chilli, garlic, ginger, spring onion and peanuts into a food processor and pulse until the mixture has bound together but the nuts are still chunky and offering some texture. Transfer the mixture to a bowl until ready to use.

2   When you are ready to fill the wontons, divide the mixture into 25 equal portions – each one should weigh 10g. Place the balls on a tray.

3   Lay 5 wonton wrappers out on a clean dry surface, angled so a corner is pointing upwards. Place a ball of filling in the middle of each one. Dip your finger into some water and lightly wet the wonton skin from 12 o'clock, to 3 o'clock and 9 o'clock respectively.

4   Take the bottom corner of the wonton skin (6 o'clock) and fold it up to meet the top corner. Gently press the wet edges together to form a seal and try to squeeze out any air pockets as you go. Next, fold the outer corners in to meet each other and seal with water.

5   Place the folded wontons on a tray and repeat the process until you have filled all the wontons. It is important the skins are not too wet, as they will stick to the tray. You can lightly dust the tray with cornflour if you are concerned the wontons are going to stick.

6   Pour the oil into a heavy-based frying pan to a depth of about 1cm. Place over a medium-high heat until it reaches a temperature of 160°C (a cube of bread should bubble and sizzle as it hits the pan). Place the wontons into the oil, being careful not to splash yourself with hot oil. Fry the wontons until brown, about 2 minutes each side, then remove from the pan and drain on kitchen paper. Do not fry all the wontons at one time, but rather fry in batches that sit comfortably in a single layer in the frying pan. Serve immediately with sticky soy for dipping.

AFTERNOON TEA

Afternoon tea (or coffee) is one of our favourite times in the restaurants. After the hum of lunch has quietened, the dining rooms are left with those enjoying that second or third bottle of wine and lingering business meetings. This makes way for a new wave and a calming transition in the rooms, the laptops come out again and the spaces are once more filled with workers, coffee drinkers and those in need of a sweet or savoury afternoon pick-me-up. Of course, our kitchen stays open all day, so any or all of these people may order something from the menu proper, or may have decided that it's the perfect time for a cocktail and a pizza. But we like to ensure that we have a couple of additional daily baked morsels to offer customers, especially those who may want to grab and go.

The recipes in this chapter definitely fall into the more decadent category, but we try to avoid highly refined sugar and sweeteners and, where we can, favour the use of unrefined golden caster sugar, whole cane sugars, raw honey, maple syrup or other natural sweeteners, such as dates. At times the use of refined caster sugar is unavoidable, as its consistency and stability is sometimes hard to match, though it is always in our minds to 'keep it clean'. However, we also value the importance of 'keeping it real' and still enjoying an occasional delicious sweet treat.

TAKE OUT DRINKS

COFFEE BLACK

ESPRESSO   2.2
LONG BLACK   2.5
FILTER   2.5

COFFEE WITH MILK

MACCHIATO   2.4
FLAT WHITE   2.8
CAPPUCCINO   2.8
LATTE   2.8

SOFTS

WATER   1.5
SODAS   3

TEA

ENGLISH BREAKFAST,
EARL GREY, ROOIBOS,   2.8
GREEN, FRESH MINT,
CAMOMILE, LEMONGRASS

FRESH JUICE

CUCUMBER, APPLE,
PARSLEY, MINT   4.5
CARROT, APPLE, GINGER,
TAMARIND   4.5

SMOOTHIE

SPIRULINA, BANANA, OAT   4.5

TAKE OUT FOOD

DAILY BAKE

MORNING BUN
SCONE
SAVOURY MUFFIN
SWEET MUFFIN
TART
BROWNIE

ROSEMARY, JAMÓN AND CHEDDAR SCONE

A warm savoury scone straight from the oven, slathered in butter, is a wonderful thing. This scone is particularly wonderful as it fills the kitchen with the delicious aromas of rosemary and jamón as they are cooking. As with any recipe like this, use it as a guide. The base scone recipe can adapt easily to accommodate other flavoursome combinations. Bacon, thyme and cheddar or feta and spinach could also work well, so feel free to experiment.

Do not overwork the scone dough once it has come together: the less you work the dough, the lighter the end result. Another tip is not to let the egg wash hit the sides of the scone – keep it on the top surface only for a more even rise.

MAKES 8–12
110g unsalted butter, chilled
140g plain flour
130g strong white bread flour
Pinch of fine sea salt
15g baking powder
120g jamón (we use Jamón de Teruel but prosciutto would work just as well)
3 rosemary sprigs, leaves stripped
85g double cream
185ml whole milk
100g Cheddar, grated
1 egg, beaten

1   Preheat the oven to 175°C and line a baking tray with baking paper.

2   In a stand mixer fitted with the paddle attachment, mix the butter and both flours to a crumb-like consistency. Add the salt and baking powder and mix together.

3   In a food processor, blend the jamón and rosemary to a fine crumb and then add to the flour mixture. Add the cream and milk and mix till just combined. Now add the cheese and mix until just combined.

4   Transfer the dough to a floured work surface and shape to a flat piece about 2cm thick. Cut into 8–12 pieces, depending on how large you like your scones.

5   Transfer to the lined baking tray and carefully brush the tops of the scones with beaten egg. Bake in the oven for 20–25 minutes.

6   Eat while still warm with lashings of butter.

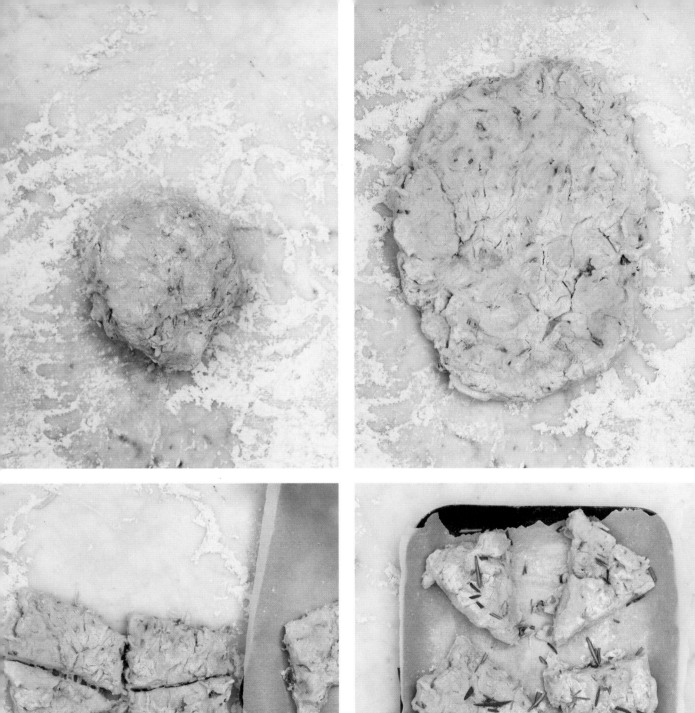

SALTED CHOCOLATE AND ALMOND BUTTER COOKIES

As with most baked goods, these are best served as soon as they come out of the oven: still gooey and with the chocolate chunks melty and soft. You can make the dough in advance and store it in the freezer; just wrap tightly in a double layer of cling film. At home, we always have a batch of dough in the freezer and pull it out when we feel like something sweet after dinner or have an afternoon tea date planned.

You'll find a recipe for almond butter in our Larder section (see page 272), but there are increasingly a growing number of good-quality, organic nut butters available, so of course feel free to use these if you don't have your own batch of almond butter to hand. Feel free to play around with other nut butters too, we've also made this recipe with cashew butter and it was equally delicious.

MAKES 12

200g unsalted butter
200g Almond Butter (see page 272 or use shop-bought)
100g muscovado sugar
50g caster sugar
2 medium eggs
2 tsp baking powder
2 tsp flaked sea salt, plus extra to finish
300g plain flour
30g good-quality cocoa powder
200g dark chocolate buttons

1   Preheat the oven to 170°C and line a large baking tray with baking paper.

2   In a stand mixer, combine the butter, almond butter and muscovado and caster sugars. Whisk on a high speed until light and fluffy, about 5 minutes.

3   Add the eggs, one at a time, beating well between each addition. Turn off the mixer and remove the bowl from the stand. Add the baking powder, sea salt, flour and cocoa powder and mix together gently with a wooden spoon. Finally fold through the chocolate buttons.

4   Divide the mixture into 12 equal parts and roll each part into a ball; place on the lined baking tray, spaced out as they will spread as they cook. Flatten each ball lightly with the palm of your hand so it is about 2cm high. Bake the cookies for 12–14 minutes.

5   Remove from the oven and sprinkle over a little extra sea salt. Transfer to a wire rack to cool.

6   These will keep for up to 1 week in an airtight container.

CHOCOLATE, ESPRESSO AND HAZELNUT BROWNIE

Over the years we have produced countless versions of the chocolate brownie. They are particularly popular in our restaurants and on our takeout counters in the afternoon, when customers seem to like a little indulgence with their coffee. We have given them an extra hit of energy by adding espresso to the mix; you can of course omit this, but we urge you to give it a try as we think it adds great flavour to the final result.

MAKES 9–12
240g unsalted butter
320g dark chocolate
4 medium eggs
400g caster sugar
80g plain flour
100ml espresso, cooled (optional)
125g hazelnuts, toasted and smashed or roughly chopped

1   Preheat the oven to 150°C and butter and line a 20cm square baking tin, at least 3cm high, with baking paper.

2   Place the butter and chocolate in a heatproof bowl and set over a pan of barely simmering water, making sure the bottom of the bowl doesn't touch the water. Mix together until melted, then set aside to cool to room temperature.

3   In a stand mixer fitted with the whisk attachment, whisk together the eggs and sugar on medium speed until the mixture has doubled in volume and is a pale colour. Let the mixture rest for 5 minutes and then bang the bowl a couple of times on the work surface to knock out some air.

4   Add the flour to the mixing bowl and fold in by hand until all the flour is mixed in. Add the cooled chocolate mixture and cooled espresso, if using, to the bowl and fold through until completely combined. Finally fold the hazelnuts through the mixture and pour into the prepared tin.

5   Before placing in the oven, drop the baking tin a couple of times onto your work surface to knock our further air. Bake for 30–35 minutes until an inserted skewer comes out with mixture on it, but the mixture is warm to the touch. Remove from the oven and leave in the tray to cool.

6   You can eat this the same day but for a super-fudgy brownie (which we love and is how we serve them at our restaurants), leave the brownie in the tray in the fridge overnight and cut into squares the following morning.

ORANGE AND ALMOND TEACAKE

We have been making this cake for years. It is so easy and everyone loves it. We have made it with clementines, blood clementines, blood oranges and pretty much every type of orange – all with great results. We always used to make it round but we are currently having a loaf moment – it works just as well and has been a happy resident on our takeout counters for some time now.

In the restaurants, we place finely sliced oranges on top of the cake, sprinkle them with sugar and then caramelise with a blowtorch; it's just for presentation but it does looks great.

MAKES I LOAF
2 small oranges
olive oil, for greasing
185g unrefined golden caster sugar
4 large eggs
185g ground almonds
¾ tsp baking powder
Crème fraîche, yoghurt or honey,
to serve

1   Remove any green stalks from the oranges and place them whole and unpeeled into a pan. Cover with water, bring to the boil and then reduce the heat and simmer for 2 hours, making sure you top up the water from time to time so that the oranges are always covered.

2   Remove the oranges from the water and put them into a food processor, skins and all. Blend to a paste and then transfer to a bowl – you need about 375g purée. Set aside.

3   Preheat the oven to 160°C. Line a 23 × 13 × 7cm loaf tin with baking paper and brush with olive oil.

4   Blend the sugar and eggs in the food processor (no need to clean the bowl) for about 1 minute until thick and creamy.

5   Add the orange purée, almonds and baking powder and pulse to combine. Do not over mix; you only need it to be just combined.

6   Pour the mixture into the lined loaf tin and then bake for 1½ hours. Remove from the oven and allow the loaf to cool in the tin for about 5 minutes. Carefully remove the loaf from the tin, remove the paper and serve with crème fraîche, yoghurt, honey or whatever tickles your fancy.

7   This cake will keep in an airtight container, at room temperature or in the fridge, for up to 5 days.

SWEET POTATO AND CINNAMON TEACAKE

This is the perfect teacake to make in the winter months as you can use any squash, pumpkin or sweet potato. The combination of the earthy sweet potato and buttermilk gives the cake a rich, tangy sweetness. This delicious, spicy cake goes perfectly with a cup of tea (or coffee!) in the afternoon.

MAKES I LOAF
3 medium or 2 large sweet potatoes
(about 250g)
225g plain flour
1½ tsp baking powder
1 tsp bicarbonate of soda
½ tsp salt
1 tbsp ground cinnamon
1 tsp ground ginger
½ tsp ground nutmeg
180ml rapeseed oil or other
neutral- flavoured oil
50ml buttermilk
250g unrefined golden caster sugar
3 large eggs

1   Preheat the oven to 180°C and line a 23 × 13 × 7cm loaf tin with baking paper.

2   Pierce the skin of the sweet potatoes with a fork a couple of times, place on a baking tray and bake for 1–1¼ hours, turning halfway through cooking. You want a completely soft potato that will be of a purée consistency. Scoop the flesh out into a bowl and discard the skins. Reduce the oven temperature to 170°C.

3   In a large mixing bowl, combine the flour, baking powder, bicarbonate of soda, salt, cinnamon, ginger and nutmeg.

4   Place the sweet potato, oil, buttermilk and caster sugar into a stand mixer fitted with the whisk attachment and mix on medium speed until you have a smooth purée. Add the eggs one at a time, beating well between each addition.

5   Now add the dry ingredients and mix on slow speed, just until a smooth batter is formed. Do not overwork the mixture.

6   Pour the batter into the lined loaf tin and bake for 1 hour. You can check to see whether the loaf is cooked by piercing it with a wooden skewer. If it comes out clean, the teacake is cooked.

7   Remove the teacake from the oven and allow it to cool for 5–10 minutes in the tin. Then remove from the tin and let it cool on a wire rack.

8   This is best eaten the same day, but will keep for at least 3 days in an airtight container or in the fridge. Make sure you bring it up to room temperature before serving.

DARK CHOCOLATE AND MISO CARAMEL WITH TOASTED SESAME SEEDS

This recipe was inspired by a trip to Japan, where we found an amazing shop that served only caramels. They were the most exquisite little paper-wrapped parcels of all different flavours, packaged in such a beautiful way, as is often the case in Japan, where aesthetics are part of the fabric of society. The caramel shop didn't, in fact, have a miso-sesame version, so this is our ode to Japan and its beauty by way of the sweetest, softest little morsels. Store this in the fridge and serve it cold, as it can get a little melty in your fingers due to the high chocolate content.

MAKES 28 BITE-SIZED PIECES

100ml double cream
250g caster sugar
100ml water
150g dark chocolate, finely chopped
50g miso paste (we use shiro
or white miso paste)
40g sesame seeds, toasted

1   Line a 23 × 13 × 7cm loaf tin with baking paper and brush lightly with a neutral vegetable oil.

2   Heat the cream in a small pan to scalding point (just before it comes to the boil) and then turn off the heat.

3   Meanwhile put the caster sugar and water in a separate small pan and place over a medium heat and bring to the boil. Continue to cook the sugar until it starts to colour, swirling the pan from time to time to evenly distribute the coloured parts of sugar with the rest.

4   As the caramel reaches a dark amber colour (at around 175°C, if you have a sugar thermometer), remove it from the heat and allow to stand for a minute before pouring in the warm cream (be careful as the cream may bubble and sputter). Return the pan to the heat and boil for 2 minutes. Again remove from the heat and stir in the chocolate and then the miso.

5   Once all is combined, carefully pour the caramel into the lined loaf tin and sprinkle over the sesame seeds. Set aside to cool and then place in the fridge overnight.

6   Turn out onto a chopping board and cut into 3cm squares. If you want to, wrap the individual caramels in baking paper. Store in the fridge for up to 2 weeks.

BANANA AND COCONUT STREUSEL CAKE AKA COFFEE CAKE

This cake is inspired by 1950s America, when most self-respecting households would have a coffee cake available for guests at all times. We felt as a self-respecting coffee house and roastery that we should also have a coffee cake in our repertoire. The use of the bundt cake tin definitely gives this cake the necessary retro feel, as does the optional glaze. We also decided to add a streusel as is common in Germany, another country with a rich tradition of coffee cakes and coffee houses. The walnut streusel adds a delicious crunchy sweet layer and a lovely look when you slice it as it snakes its way around the centre of the cake.

MAKES I CAKE

175g unsalted butter,
at room temperature
300g unrefined golden caster sugar
3 large eggs, at room temperature
1½ tsp vanilla extract
275ml buttermilk or sour cream
250g plain flour
50g desiccated coconut
2 tsp baking powder
½ tsp bicarbonate of soda
½ tsp fine sea salt
2 large ripe bananas, mashed

STREUSEL

35g coconut palm sugar
50g plain flour
1½ tsp ground cinnamon
¼ tsp fine sea salt
30g unsalted butter, chilled
and diced
60g walnuts, finely chopped

GLAZE (OPTIONAL)

140g icing sugar
3 tbsp coconut milk or whole milk,
plus more if needed
2 tsp lemon juice

1   Preheat the oven to 170°C and butter a bundt cake tin.

2   In a stand mixer, cream the butter and sugar until light, around 4–5 minutes. Add the eggs one at a time, mixing well between each addition. Now add the vanilla and buttermilk or sour cream and mix to combine.

3   In a medium bowl combine the flour, coconut, baking powder, bicarbonate of soda and salt and whisk to remove any lumps. Add this flour mixture to the batter in the stand mixer and mix on low speed until combined. Finally fold in the mashed bananas to combine.

4   To make the streusel, put the coconut palm sugar, flour, cinnamon and salt in a medium bowl. Add the diced butter and then pinch and squeeze the ingredients together until they form a crumble. Now add the walnuts and rub into the crumble.

5   Sprinkle half the streusel mixture into the bottom of the bundt tin and press down firmly with your hands. Pour half the batter over the streusel and spread evenly with a cake slice or knife. Sprinkle the remaining streusel evenly over the batter, then pour in the remainder of the batter.

6   Bake for 50–60 minutes or until a wooden skewer inserted into the centre comes out clean. Remove from the oven and allow to cool in the tin for 10 minutes before turning out onto a wire rack to cool completely.

7   To make the glaze, sift the icing sugar into a bowl and gradually add the milk, stirring as you go. Next stir in the lemon juice; you want a pourable consistency that is not too thin, so add more milk if you need to. Drizzle over the cooled cake so that it falls down the indents. Allow to set for at least 30 minutes, then serve with a cup of Caravan coffee.

8   This will last in an airtight container at room temperature for up to 3 days.

DINNER: SEAFOOD & MEAT

In New Zealand you are never very far from the coast, and never very far from a farm. In fact, most major cities and small towns are built right on the coast, meaning the ocean and its bounty is an intrinsic part of our culinary heritage. Likewise, we are fortunate to have enough space for high-quality meat production, while retaining huge swathes of native bush, mountain ranges and coastal boarders. A good roast followed by a bracing bush walk is a national pastime. We all fondly remember childhoods that revolved around eating fish straight from the ocean, especially summer holidays at the beach house, and celebrating many a happy occasion with slow-roasted lamb or meat and seafood straight off the barbecue.

Happily, living and owning restaurants in the UK has not resulted in any less of a celebration surrounding beautifully sourced, fresh seafood and meat. When we first moved here, over 16 years ago, we got very excited by the new fish varieties and crustacea to explore and conducted many a taste test on whether salt marsh Welsh lamb was better than New Zealand lamb (both are totally delicious, of course). And although we consciously focus on vegetable and grain dishes at the restaurants, our menus would not be complete without the inclusion of seasonal, well sourced and sustainable fish and meat.

We are all becoming more aware of the provenance, environmental impact and rearing practices used in the fishing and meat industries. Our approach at the restaurants is to only use fish and meat from reliable and sustainable sources. We feel it is our duty as chefs and restaurateurs to take this concern from the customers and we do it with pleasure.

Of course, we know it is not always possible for you to spend the same amount of time as we do sourcing your fresh fish and meat. Wherever possible we encourage you to buy from your local butcher or fishmonger, who is in turn hopefully supplying locally sourced, seasonal fish and meat, or to make use of a local farmers' market for your weekly fish and meat quota. Budget can be an obstacle when sourcing good-quality fish and meat, but by buying ingredients when they are truly in season and using cheaper cuts, such as oxtail, ham hock, brisket, pork belly, ribs and shoulder, hopefully your purse can stretch and your conscience will thank you for it too.

The seafood recipes in this chapter are an international mix of origins and flavours. We use a lot of Asian ingredients in our seafood recipes, as they complement so harmoniously the delicate flavours. Feel free to play around with some of these ingredients, sauces and condiments and don't be put off if you are missing one or two of them — many can be replaced with an alternative and will still create a beautiful dish.

The meat recipes are equally globally inspired, this time with an emphasis on North African, Middle Eastern and Mediterranean ingredients. In many cases, we have paired the meat with a starch and vegetables as part of the recipe, but feel free to create your own feasts using as many grains, leaves and vegetables as you can to add to the mix.

TEMPURA OYSTERS WITH CITRUS MAYONNAISE

Growing up in New Zealand, no order of fish and chips was complete without a dozen deep-fried oysters; as a result we are all obsessed with them. There is something just so delicious about the flavours of a salty, fresh oyster combined with crisp batter. From late March to early August, the best on offer are fat juicy native Bluff oysters, which are grown in the wild clean waters of the Foveaux Strait – the body of water that runs between New Zealand's South Island and Stewart Island. In trying to recreate this memory from childhood, we look for the fattest, firmest oysters on the market. Whether you choose natives or rocks, make sure they are really fresh and as big as you can find. We think the perfect batter to use is a tempura style as it is light and crisps up really well, meaning the oysters do not get lost in a thick, stodgy batter.

SERVES 4
80g cornflour
220g plain flour
200ml sparkling water
4–5 ice cubes
16 native oysters, shucked
Rapeseed oil, for frying

TO SERVE
Citrus Mayonnaise (see page 274)
Lime wedges
Flaked sea salt (smoked sea salt is great, if you have it)

1   Mix the cornflour and 100g of the plain flour together in a medium bowl. Add the sparkling water and ice cubes and use two chopsticks to mix from the centre out until flour and water are incorporated (a lumpy mixture is fine). Set aside to rest for at least 10 minutes.

2   Shuck your oysters and lay them out on kitchen paper, checking carefully to remove any pieces of shell.

3   When you are ready to cook, heat the oil in your deep fryer to 170°C. (Alternatively, see page 288 for instructions on how to fry without a deep fryer.)

4   Just before using give the tempura batter another stir with the chopsticks. Place the remaining flour in a small bowl and individually dust the oysters in the flour. Working quickly, use tongs or chopsticks to dip the floured oysters into the tempura batter; remove and immediately dip into the hot oil, holding the oysters just below the surface of the oil until the batter swells and hits the top of the oil. Then you can release the oyster into the oil. Deep-fry each one for 3–4 minutes until crispy and pale – you do not want the batter to turn brown. Remove from the fryer and place on a dish lined with kitchen paper. The size of your fryer or pan will determine how many oysters you can cook at a time; do not overload the pan, as they will stick together.

5   Repeat until all the oysters are cooked. Serve with citrus mayonnaise on the side and a sprinkle of sea salt.

SCALLOP CEVICHE WITH AVOCADO PURÉE, NORI AND TOASTED BUCKWHEAT

While I love a scallop cooked straight on the barbecue and dressed simply with lemon juice and pepper, I fell in love with raw scallops as my palate developed. They are so creamy and delicate. They are also very rich, which means a little goes a long way. In truth, I never leave the scallops in the acidic juice for very long, but prefer them lightly dressed just before serving; whether this is technically a ceviche is up for debate but I call it that so people understand what it is. You can find shiso leaves at specialist Asian supermarkets or online, but they can also be substituted for mint and/or coriander cress. (MK)

SERVES 4
1 avocado, flesh blended
to a smooth purée
1 tbsp yuzu juice (or use
lemon juice)
1 tsp fine sea salt
20ml soy sauce
20ml mirin
20ml rice wine vinegar
10ml truffle oil
1 nori sheet
4 large king scallops, coral
removed, patted dry
½ tbsp toasted buckwheat
Few shiso leaves (or use mint
or coriander cress)

1   Combine the avocado purée, yuzu juice and sea salt in a small bowland stir well to amalgamate (to get it really smooth, blend in a liquidiser or high-speed smoothie maker). Set aside.

2   Combine the soy, mirin, vinegar and truffle oil in a separate bowl and set aside.

3   Toast your nori sheet over a gas flame on your stove. Do this by using kitchen tongs to hold the nori sheet directly over the flame; turn it regularly to achieve an evenly toasted and crisp sheet of nori that will crumble when you crush it in your hand. Avoid using pieces that are too dark from the cooking process, as they will have taken on a bitter flavour. The nori should be crisp and dull in colour.

4   Use a sharp knife to slice the scallops into thin slices, about 2–3mm thick. Place in the bowl with the soy sauce, mirin and rice wine vinegar. Allow it to stand for a few minutes, while you dress the plates.

5   Using the back of a spoon spread the avocado purée roughly over your serving plates. Lay the dressed slices of scallop on top of the avocado purée and spoon on any extra dressing from the bowl.

6   Top the plate with the crumbled nori, toasted buckwheat and a sprinkling of shiso leaves.

FENNEL AND MISO CURED SALMON

The great thing about this cure is that you get varying degrees of flavour and intensity, depending on what part of the salmon you are eating. The tail end, which is thinner, will be saltier and more flavourful, while slices from the middle of the fillet will be less intense and have a subtler cure flavour. Cured salmon is a wonderful thing to have in your fridge as it can be used in so many ways: on its own with a simple slice of soda bread or toasted sourdough, with scrambled eggs and chives for breakfast or as a starter with shaved cucumber and fennel.

MAKES 20 SLICES
(SERVES 6 AS A STARTER)
100g fine sea salt
100g unrefined golden caster sugar
1 tbsp fennel seeds, toasted
½ fennel bulb, roughly chopped
100g white miso paste
1kg whole salmon fillet, skinned and trimmed
Small handful of chopped dill

1   Place the salt, caster sugar, fennel seeds, fennel and miso paste in a food processor and pulse until the fennel has broken down.

2   Lay a large, double layer of cling film on your work surface. Spoon half the curing mix onto the cling film and place the salmon fillet on top. Spread the rest of the curing mixture evenly on top of the salmon. Wrap the salmon tightly in the cling film – if it begins to leak, wrap another layer of cling film around it. Place in the fridge to cure for at least 48 hours.

3   Remove from the fridge and unwrap the salmon. Wipe off the cure and then pat dry with kitchen paper to remove any excess curing mixture. Place the salmon onto a chopping board and cut into about 20 pieces, each about 3mm thick, cutting straight across the salmon. Sprinkle with some freshly chopped dill and serve.

4   If left unsliced, the salmon will keep in the fridge for up to 1 week.

PICKLED MACKEREL WITH YUZU AND SHALLOTS

Our interest in pickling fish came from a stint living in the Netherlands, where the pickled 'haring' is a national obsession. It is also borne out of an increasing concern not be wasteful with any ingredient, especially seafood, and pickling is a great way of doing this. This dish is more a take on the South African style of pickling (with some not so traditional ingredients added for good measure), in which the fish is cooked first then pickled. It is not the sort of pickle that will keep for months, but it can be prepared a couple of days in advance. We feel it is definitely at its best one day after it is made. If left too long, the fish can 'over-pickle' and the texture can be compromised. It will keep for 5–7 days.

SERVES 6
½ tsp fine sea salt
200g plain flour
1 tbsp coriander seeds, toasted
and crushed
1 tbsp black mustard seeds
6 skin-on mackerel fillets,
pin-boned
4 tbsp rapeseed or other
neutral-flavoured oil, for frying
4 shallots, halved lengthways
and sliced
4 garlic cloves, sliced
2 bay leaves
4 tbsp yuzu juice (you can find this
at most good supermarkets,
or substitute a mixture of lemon
and grapefruit juice)
2 tbsp light soy sauce
150ml apple cider vinegar
1 tsp unrefined golden caster sugar
300ml olive oil (or enough to cover)

1   Combine the salt, flour and coriander and mustard seeds in a shallow tray and then dust the mackerel fillets on both sides with the seasoned flour.

2   Heat 2 tablespoons of the oil in large frying pan and fry the mackerel until golden brown on each side; remove from the pan and set aside in a high-sided, heat-proof dish.

3   Heat the remaining oil in a separate pan and add the shallots, garlic and bay leaves. Cook over a medium heat until soft. Remove from the heat and add the yuzu juice, soy sauce, vinegar and sugar and stir to combine.

4   Pour the shallot liquid over the mackerel, top with olive oil to cover and refrigerate for at least 2 hours before serving. This is delicious with a few simple salad leaves; in the restaurant we serve it with wasabi-flavoured crème fraîche and toasted buckwheat.

COD CEVICHE WITH COCONUT, CORIANDER AND LIME

Anywhere in the world where there is an abundance of fresh fish, people like to eat it raw or lightly marinated. We were lucky enough to enjoy a lot of fresh fish growing up in New Zealand and this recipe is inspired by our neighbours in the Pacific Islands. If you are unable find taro, use sweet potato as an alternative. Physalis can be replaced with mango, tomato or papaya. This recipe would also work well with sea bass, grouper or stone bass.

SERVES 4–6 AS A STARTER
30g fresh ginger, peeled and very finely chopped
1 small garlic clove, very finely chopped
120ml lime juice
½ tsp sea salt
60g coriander stalks, chopped
400ml coconut milk
200g taro or sweet potato, peeled and cut into 1cm chunks
400g very fresh cod, cut into 2cm chunks
½ medium red onion, shaved
2 spring onions, thinly sliced
20g coriander leaves
100g physalis, peeled and quartered
20 Taro Crisps (see page 289)

1   Put the ginger, garlic, lime juice, sea salt, coriander stalks and coconut milk into a food processor or blender and blitz until combined. Allow the mixture to stand for 15 minutes then pass through a fine sieve and place in the fridge until ready to use.

2   Bring a medium pan of water to the boil. Once the water is boiling, drop in the diced taro or sweet potato and cook until soft through; this will take around 10 minutes. Drain and allow it to cool before you use it.

3   Fifteen minutes before serving, place the diced cod in a mixing bowl with the coconut dressing and allow it to stand for 10 minutes. Stir it gently every couple of minutes to make sure the fish is evenly coated in the dressing.

4   Add the diced taro or sweet potato, red onion, spring onions, coriander and physalis and again gently stir the contents of the bowl to dress everything evenly. Spoon the mixture onto a serving platter and top with the taro crisps.

MUSSELS WITH CHORIZO, OLOROSO AND PARSLEY

Full of flavour and quick and easy to prepare, this is one of our favourite dishes to cook when fresh mussels are at their best during the winter months. The chorizo and sherry create a warming wintery broth that is perfect for mopping up with crusty bread. Before you cook your mussels, pick through them carefully to find and discard any that are already open. You should only use the mussels that are firmly shut, indicating they are still alive. After you have cooked them, discard any that have not opened in the cooking process.

To remove the beards from the mussels, use a tea towel or other kitchen cloth to get a firm grip on the beard that appears from the gap at the bottom of the shell and gently pull on the beard as you slide it upwards. The beard should release from the mussel relatively easily but it takes a little practice to get the knack.

SERVES 4
50ml olive oil
1 shallot, roughly diced
2 garlic cloves, thinly sliced
200g cooking chorizo, peeled and roughly chopped
1kg live mussels, scrubbed and beards removed
100ml Oloroso sherry
Handful of flat-leaf parsley, roughly chopped
Crusty bread, to serve

1   Heat the olive oil in large heavy-based pan and fry the shallot and garlic over a medium heat until just coloured. Add the chorizo and stir until it releases some of its delicious oils.

2   Add the mussels to the pan and stir to coat the mussels in the oil. Pour in the sherry and immediately place a lid on the pan and turn up the heat. Steam the mussels for 3–6 minutes until all the mussels have opened.

3   Just before serving, stir through the parsley and then pour the mussels onto a serving dish. Eat with your fingers and mop up any excess juice with some crusty bread.

CLAMS WITH GARLIC, CHILLI, PARSLEY AND LEMON

There are a few things you should know before you cook clams. Clams should be tightly closed and they should smell of the ocean or seaweed, rather than smelling strongly of fish, so discard any that do not fit this profile, as well as any that have broken or damaged shells. If you find any with open shells, lightly tap the shell; if the clam is alive, the shell will close tightly and can be used. Once they are cooked the opposite applies: discard any clams that remain firmly closed.

This recipe is quick and simple to prepare and lets the sweet clams do all the talking. Serve with a bowl of angel hair pasta or spaghetti seasoned with good-quality olive oil, sea salt flakes and freshly cracked pepper. Or they are simply delicious on their own as a starter with chunks of crusty bread to mop up the juices.

SERVES 4
50ml olive oil
1 shallot, roughly diced
1kg palourde clams, washed well in cold running water
½ large red chilli, deseeded and roughly diced
2 garlic cloves, thinly sliced
1 lemon, thinly sliced into rounds
100ml white wine
Small handful of flat-leaf parsley, roughly chopped
Fine sea salt

1   Heat the olive oil in a large heavy-based pan and fry the shallot over a medium heat until just coloured.

2   Add the clams and stir to coat with the shallots. Next add the chilli, garlic and sliced lemon and cook for 2–3 minutes. Now add the wine. Cover the pan and cook for 5–8 minutes or until the clams have opened.

3   Add the parsley, season with salt to taste and serve immediately, with plenty of bread to mop up the delicious juices.

CRISP-SKINNED SEA BASS WITH GREEN MANGO SOM TAM

This is a real crowd-pleaser. There is something special about serving a whole fish to guests and letting them get stuck in to help themselves. Somehow people are less wasteful when they see a whole fish in front of them and I find they are more appreciative of what they are eating than when it is a perfect portion sliced from a fillet.

At home, we eat this in the summer and barbecue the fish. Growing up, we would always grill over driftwood from the beach. In London, we use good-quality, sustainable charcoal. The results are slightly different but the enjoyment is the same. If you are unable to source green mango or green papaya, you can substitute cucumber, kohlrabi or courgette for one or both.

SERVES 4
2 whole sea bass (about 500g each), gutted, scaled and fins removed
¼ tsp fine sea salt
¼ tsp cracked black pepper
Rapeseed oil, for frying (optional)

SOM TAM SALAD
60g coriander (leaves and stalks), chopped
½ tsp fine sea salt
1 garlic clove, smashed
5g fresh ginger, chopped
1–2 red chillies, sliced
20g palm sugar (or use caster sugar)
60g ripe cherry tomatoes, halved
1 tbsp nam pla (fish sauce)
3 tbsp lime juice
2 tsp tamarind juice
100g green mango, finely sliced (or use cucumber)
100g green papaya, finely sliced (or use red cabbage)
4–5 spring onions, sliced
Small handful of coriander leaves
50g peanuts, roasted and crushed

1 First make the som tam salad. Pound the coriander, salt, garlic, ginger and half the chilli to a paste with a mortar and pestle. Add the palm sugar and pound until dissolved, then add the tomatoes and roughly pound to release all the juice.

2 Add the fish sauce, lime juice and tamarind juice and mix with a spoon to combine. Set aside.

3 Place the green mango, green papaya, spring onions, coriander leaves, remaining chilli and peanuts in a large bowl and pour the dressing over. Gently turn the salad to make sure every part is dressed well. Set aside.

TO COOK ON THE BARBECUE

4 At least 30 minutes before you wish to cook the sea bass, prepare your barbecue. Light the coals and allow the flames to burn out and the coals to achieve a consistent heat – the outer layer of the coal will be white at this stage. Ensure the coals are evenly spread on the base of the barbecue, leaving one corner without any coals.

5 Lay the fish flat on a chopping board and on each side, make 4 cuts ½ cm deep, through the skin and into the flesh, and sprinkle the salt and pepper on to both sides of the skin.

6 If you have a fish cage for barbecuing, place the fish inside this and place the cage directly onto the grill. The cage will allow you to move the fish around if the coals are too hot without the skin sticking to the grill. Alternatively, you can barbecue the fish directly onto the grill, but be careful to ensure that the heat is not too intense before placing the fish on the grill as the skin will burn before the fish cooks. Cook on each side for 5–6 minutes, depending on the heat of your barbecue. A good way to check that the fish is done is to gently pull the flesh away from the bone; if it comes away easily and the flesh is white, it is ready.

4   Preheat the oven to 170°C.

5   Heat a little oil in a large, ovenproof frying pan then place the fish
     into the pan. The oil should be hot enough so that the fish sizzles.
     Fry the fish over a medium heat on one side until the skin is golden
     and crispy, about 4–5 minutes.

6   Carefully flip the fish over onto the other side, fry for 2 minutes then
     place in the oven and cook for 8–10 minutes.

7   Place the cooked sea bass on a board or serving plate with the som
     tam salad in a bowl on the side. Make sure you pour out all the
     dressing from the bowl too as this will soak into the fish and make
     it delicious.

SEARED SEA TROUT, NORI PURÉE, MISO BUTTER

I first encountered nori purée when working for Peter Gordon at the Providores and Tapa Room in London's Marylebone. We were developing a vegetarian sauce for a dinner that we were doing, I can't recall why, but we needed it to be black – it may have had something to do with rugby. I tried various methods but everything came out grey. Peter worked his magic and something like this was born. This is not the exact same recipe but it comes from the same idea. (MK)

SERVES 4
2 tbsp rapeseed oil 4 × 180g skin-on pieces of boneless sea trout
Sea salt and black pepper

NORI PURÉE
8 nori sheets
100ml mirin
100ml sake
100ml soy sauce
50ml balsamic vinegar

MISO BUTTER
85g unsalted butter, at room temperature
50g white miso paste

1   First make the nori purée. Hold the nori sheets over the flame on your stove with a pair of tongs. Flip the nori over repeatedly until the sheet begins to dull in colour and crisp up. Be careful as it can burst into flames (but can be extinguished relatively easily with a light blow).

2   Set the nori to the side and when all sheets are toasted, crumble them with your fingers into a bowl.

3   Combine all the liquids in a small pan and bring to the boil, then allow to simmer for 30 seconds. Add the crumbled nori to the pan and whisk to bring it all together. Cook over a gentle heat until the liquid has all but evaporated.

4   Using a stick blender or high-speed smoothie maker, blend the mixture to a purée and set aside until needed. (This can be made in advance and will keep in the fridge for a week.)

5   To make the miso butter, mix the softened butter and miso paste together in a small bowl until completely combined. Spoon the miso butter onto a sheet of cling film and roll it up to form a wrapped sausage of butter, about 4cm long. Chill in the fridge until needed. To use, unwrap the cling film and slice into 1cm thick rounds.

6   When you are ready to cook the fish heat the oil in a non-stick pan until sizzling. Meanwhile, use a sharp knife to make 3–4 score marks through the skin of each piece of fish; season with salt and pepper. Lay each fillet skin-side down in the hot oil; it should sizzle immediately. Cook for 2–3 minutes until the skin is golden and crisp. Remove the pan from the heat and flip the fish over to the other side. Leave to sit off the heat in the warm pan for a further 2–3 minutes.

7   To serve, smear a good dollop of nori purée over 4 plates. Unwrap the miso butter and slice into 4 rounds, each 1cm thick. Place a piece of cooked fish on top of the purée and then a slice of butter on top to finish it off. This would be delicious with a simple fresh salad, or the soba noodle salad on page 118.

BRAISED OCTOPUS, MOJO VERDE, BURNT LEMON

As a youngster, when I was fishing once in the Marlborough Sounds, New Zealand, I inadvertently hooked an octopus. I let it go, partly because of my fear of getting suckered by it and partly because we really had no idea what to do with it once we got it on board the boat. This was a long time ago now and if I had a second chance with that creature on my line, given how much I love this recipe, I think its chances of survival would be pretty slim. A good local fishmonger will be able to source a lovely octopus and clean it up for you. This would pair nicely with creamy polenta (see page 76). (MK)

SERVES 4
1 large octopus, cleaned
3 lemons, 1 cut into quarters
3 bay leaves
5 garlic cloves, bashed
½ red onion
1 tbsp cracked black pepper
200g Mojo Verde (see page 281), to serve

1   Place the octopus into a large pan with the quartered lemon, bay leaves, garlic, red onion and pepper and add 200ml water. Bring to the boil, then cover with a lid, reduce the heat to low and gently simmer for around 45–50 minutes until the tentacles are tender.

2   Turn off the heat and leave the octopus to cool in the liquid. Once cool, drain off the liquid and pat the tentacles dry with kitchen paper. Set aside.

3   Light your barbecue and once the coals are ready, place the octopus right onto the grill above the hot coals. I prefer to grill the octopus whole and portion it up after it has come off the heat. If barbecuing is not an option you can char the octopus in a griddle pan – you will need a little oil in the pan to help it colour.

4   Cut the remaining 2 lemons in half and place cut side down on the barbecue directly over the hottest part of the coals; cook until blackened. This will soften the flavour of the lemon juice and make the lemon 'juicer' and easier to squeeze. (Alternatively, you can char these in the griddle pan.)

5   Once the octopus is nice and charred, place it on a chopping board. Using a sharp knife, slice off each of the tentacles and place on a serving platter or board. Dress the octopus liberally with mojo verde, and serve with the blackened lemons.

CUTTLEFISH, YUZU AND SAFFRON HOTPOT

If you are preparing this from scratch, the first thing you need to do is find a decent apron and some gloves, as there's a good chance you will get covered in ink. However, the other option is to ask your local fishmonger to clean and prepare the cuttlefish for you. Cuttlefish, not unlike its cousin the squid, likes to be cooked either hard and fast, or super slow. It is meatier than squid and we think prefers to be cooked slowly. It also has more of a propensity to take on the flavours of the things you cook with it. Yuzu and saffron has been a favourite flavour combination at Caravan for as long as we can remember. Thank you Cristian Hossack (my old sous chef from The Providores and Tapa Room) for that little gem.

This dish is best served with warm crusty bread and a green leafy salad (see page 106), or a bowl of steaming rice. (MK)

SERVES 4–6
3 tbsp olive oil
2 large brown onions, finely diced
6 garlic cloves
50g plain flour
500ml dry white wine
1 litre fish stock or water
800g cuttlefish, cut into 6cm pieces
2 bay leaves
Thumb-sized piece of unpeeled fresh ginger, sliced into 4 pieces
3 tbsp light soy sauce
½ celeriac, peeled and chopped into 3cm pieces
2 fennel bulbs, trimmed, cut vertically and then into 3cm pieces
Small handful of flat-leaf parsley, finely chopped

YUZU AND SAFFRON BUTTER
20ml yuzu juice (or use a mixture of lemon and grapefruit juice)
½ tsp saffron threads
100g unsalted butter, softened
¼ tsp fine sea salt

1   Preheat the oven to 175°C.

2   Heat the olive oil in a large casserole, add the onions and garlic and fry until the onion is translucent and the garlic is starting to brown. Sprinkle over the flour and stir to distribute evenly; fry for 2 minutes. Add the wine and continue to stir as the mixture thickens. Gradually add the fish stock or water, continuing to stir.

3   Now add the cuttlefish, bay leaves, ginger and soy sauce and bring to the boil. Cover with a tight-fitting lid and place in the oven for 1 hour.

4   Meanwhile make the yuzu and saffron butter. Place all the ingredients into a stand mixer with the whisk attachment and mix for 8–10 minutes on medium speed until the yuzu juice is integrated into the butter. Chill in the fridge until ready to use.

5   Remove the casserole from oven, add the celeriac and fennel and turn to combine. Return to the oven with the lid on for a further 30–45 minutes until the celeriac is tender when pierced with a knife.

6   When the hotpot is ready, remove from the oven and sprinkle with the chopped parsley. Dollop over 8–10 teaspoons of the yuzu and saffron butter and replace the lid for a minute to melt the butter. Serve immediately.

SWEET POTATO AND CHORIZO CROQUETTES, SAFFRON MAYONNAISE

Deciding which croquette recipe to put in the book was tough. It came down to a vote and this recipe won by a nose. We adore croquettes at Caravan and have always had them on the menus with many different variations over the years. To ensure a great result with these, make sure the sweet potato is dry after baking and not soggy. If the sweet potato appears wet, strain off any excess liquid before mixing it though the béchamel sauce and chorizo. The béchamel sauce should also be lovely and thick before using – allowing it to cool completely will make it easier to shape the croquettes.

MAKES 25 CROQUETTES
500g sweet potatoes (2–3 medium)
300g cooking chorizo, skinned
50g butter
50g plain flour, plus extra
for dusting
400ml whole milk
2 spring onions, thinly sliced
5 eggs, lightly whisked
Panko breadcrumbs, for crumbing
Rapeseed oil, for deep-frying
Sea salt and black pepper
Saffron Aioli (see page 274),
to serve

1   Preheat the oven to 170°C, then place the sweet potatoes on a roasting tray and bake in their skins for about 40 minutes, or until soft all the way through. Allow to cool and then cut them in half lengthways and scoop out the flesh. Mash the flesh with a fork and set aside (you should get about 250g mashed sweet potato).

2   Meanwhile place the chorizo in another roasting tray or ovenproof pan and roast in the same oven for about 10 minutes. Allow to cool then place in a food processor and pulse until the chorizo is the texture of very coarse crumbs. Set aside.

3   Melt the butter in a medium pan over a low heat. Remove from the heat and tip in the flour, then return to a medium heat and stir continuously for around 4 minutes to 'cook out' the flour. Remove the pan from the heat and pour in half the milk; it will bubble and thicken immediately, so keep stirring to avoid any lumps forming. Add the remaining milk to the pan, return to a low heat and continue to stir as the mixture thickens. Cook for 4–5 minutes to produce a thick white sauce that will make up the base for the croquettes. Set aside to cool completely.

4   In a large bowl, mix together the chorizo, 250g sweet potato mash and the white sauce until all is combined. Add the spring onions, season with salt and pepper and mix again.

5   Set 3 large bowls out in front of you on the work surface: some flour for dusting in one, the beaten egg in another and the panko breadcrumbs in the third. Use a set of scales to weigh out 25 × 30g balls then roll them in the bowl of flour and toss to make sure they get an even coating. Dip each floured ball in the beaten egg and then roll in the crumbs. Place all the crumbed croquettes in a single layer on a large tray and chill in the fridge until ready to fry.

6   If you have a deep fryer, turn it on and heat the oil to 170°C. Fry the croquettes in batches for about 4–5 minutes until golden and crispy – do not overcrowd the pan. If you do not have a deep fryer, see the deep-frying notes on page 288. Remove with a slotted spoon, drain on kitchen paper and serve hot, with saffron aioli.

FRIED CHICKEN WITH WATERMELON AND POMEGRANATE MOLASSES

This is our take on an American favourite. The chicken recipe itself is a combination of a Southern fried version and a Japanese karaage recipe. The watermelon salad is designed to cleanse the palate, with the pomegranate molasses giving the watermelon a tart kick. If you don't have pomegranate molasses, simply dress the watermelon with some fresh lemon juice. The leg meat is always the best when it comes to frying chicken, it does not dry out like breast meat can.

SERVES 4
20ml soy sauce
1 tsp sesame oil
2 tsp rice wine vinegar
200g crème fraîche
3 garlic cloves, very finely chopped
Small thumb-sized piece of fresh ginger, very finely chopped
10 boneless chicken thighs, skin on
100g plain flour
30g garlic powder
1 tbsp smoked paprika
1 tbsp black sesame seeds
½ tsp fine sea salt
Vegetable oil, for frying

WATERMELON SALAD
35ml pomegranate molasses
15ml olive oil
½ tsp cracked black pepper
600g watermelon, cut into 6cm chunks
Small handful of basil leaves
Small handful of mint leaves
15 chives, cut in 2cm batons
Handful pomegranate seeds (optional)

1   Combine the soy sauce, sesame oil, rice wine vinegar, crème fraîche, garlic and ginger in a medium bowl and stir to combine. Cut the chicken thighs in half and add to the bowl. Cover tightly with cling film and place in the fridge to marinate for at least 1 hour, or up to 12 hours.

2   Meanwhile, prepare the watermelon salad. Whisk the pomegranate molasses, olive oil and pepper together in a bowl. Add the watermelon and toss to coat in the dressing and let stand for 5 minutes. Combine the herbs in a separate bowl and set aside.

3   Combine the flour, garlic powder, smoked paprika, sesame seeds and sea salt in a large shallow bowl and set aside.

4   Remove the chicken from the fridge. Lift the pieces of chicken from the marinade and place into the flour mixture in preparation for frying.

5   Heat enough vegetable oil in a heavy-based frying pan to come about 1cm up the sides of the pan. When it reaches 170°C (a few crumbs dropped in the pan should sizzle immediately), carefully place pieces of floured chicken into the oil, making sure the hot oil does not splash on you.

6   Fry the chicken in batches until brown all over and cooked all the way through. This will take about 5 minutes on each side but will depend on the temperature of the oil and the size of the chicken pieces. Remove from the pan and drain on kitchen paper to dry off the excess cooking oil.

7   Pour the watermelon and all the dressing onto a serving plate, pile the mixed herbs on top and sprinkle with pomegranate seeds (if using). Serve immediately with the hot fried chicken.

RARE ROAST SIRLOIN WITH POPPED CAPERS AND ANCHOVY-TARRAGON DRESSING

We have gone for a beef recipe where a few slices per person is enough for everyone to enjoy when paired with some lovely vegetables, a salad, some Puy lentils or polenta as part of a feast. This started life as a small plate on our menus but for home, it translates to a fantastic centrepiece for a lunch or dinner party coupled with lots of other yummy things.

SERVES 6
1kg beef sirloin
Fine sea salt and black pepper
Few tarragon leaves, to garnish

POPPED CAPERS
40g capers
200ml rapeseed oil

ANCHOVY-TARRAGON DRESSING
10–15 anchovies, roughly chopped
50g shallots, very finely diced
50ml extra-virgin olive oil
20ml red wine vinegar
2 garlic cloves, grated
1 tbsp Dijon mustard
Small handful of tarragon leaves, chopped
1 tsp cracked black pepper

1   Preheat the oven to 200°C.

2   Season the beef generously with salt and pepper and then place into a large frying pan, fat side down, and place over a low heat. Leave the beef fat side down for at least 20 minutes to render as much fat as possible; the remaining fat on the beef should turn brown and crispy.

3   Increase the heat to medium and brown all the remaining sides of the sirloin, about 3–5 minutes each side. Transfer to a roasting tray and then roast in the oven for 20–25 minutes, or until the centre reaches 50°C if you have a meat thermometer. Remove from the oven and set aside to rest on your work surface for at least 15 minutes, loosely covered in foil.

4   While the meat is resting, 'pop' the capers. Drain away any liquid from the capers and pat them dry on kitchen paper. Heat the oil in a pan over a medium heat and carefully add the capers. They will spit and 'hiss' at you until all the moisture has evaporated. Once the hissing stops, carefully remove the crisp capers from the oil with a slotted spoon and drain on kitchen paper. Set aside to cool.

5   Place all the ingredients for the dressing in a small bowl and mix together until combined.

6   Carve the beef to the desired thickness and arrange the slices on a board or serving plate. Drizzle the anchovy dressing over the top and then scatter over the popped capers. Finally top with some whole tarragon leaves and serve.

CHARGRILLED LAMB CUTLETS, CHERMOULA

These lamb cutlets are best cooked on a charcoal barbecue; it evokes strong memories for us of the charcoal grills at the night market in Marrakesh. When paired with the chermoula, it's like you are there. But of course a gas barbecue, griddle or inside chargrill will do the trick too.

In New Zealand, when someone says 'chur', it is an exclamation and recognition of the positive nature of a situation, comment or product. When I prepared chermoula with Iain and Dallas from legendary New Zealand band Fat Freddy's Drop for the launch of their album Blackbird, they liked it so much they started calling it 'chur-moula'. This was a great compliment and has been referred to as 'chur-moula' in our kitchens ever since. (MK)

SERVES 4
12 lamb cutlets
100ml vegetable oil
Sea salt and black pepper

CHERMOULA
1 cinnamon stick
1 tbsp cumin seeds
1 tbsp coriander seeds
½ tsp saffron threads
1 small red onion, finely diced
1 small garlic clove, very finely chopped or grated
1 mild red chilli, deseeded and finely chopped
1 tbsp smoked paprika
1 tbsp Preserved Lemon rind (see page 285 or use shop-bought), finely chopped
90ml lemon juice
200ml extra-virgin olive oil
Handful of flat-leaf parsley leaves, roughly chopped
Handful of coriander (leaves and tender stalks), roughly chopped
Sea salt and black pepper

1   First prepare the chermoula – you can do this ahead as it will keep for up to a week in the fridge. Break the cinnamon into small pieces with your hands and toast over a medium heat in a heavy-based pan for about 3–5 minutes. Once fragrant and toasted, place in a mortar and pound to a fine powder. Tip into a mixing bowl. Toast the cumin and coriander seeds in the same way, until they are turning brown and smell fragrant. Remove the pan from the heat and add the saffron to the warm pan (this will intensify the flavour and colour of the saffron). Gently pound the seeds and the saffron, just to break up the seeds. Pour these into the bowl with the cinnamon.

2   Add the red onion, garlic, chilli, smoked paprika, preserved lemon, lemon juice and olive oil to the bowl and mix together. Stir through the chopped herbs and season to taste with salt and pepper.

3   At least 30 minutes before you wish to cook, prepare your barbecue. Light the coals and allow the flames to burn out and the coals to achieve a consistent heat – the outer layer of the coal will be white at this stage. Ensure the coals are evenly spread on the base of the barbecue, leaving one corner without any coals. This empty portion of the barbecue will offer a welcome escape area for any food caramelising or burning too quickly.

4   Once the barbecue is ready to go, place the lamb chops in a bowl or on a tray and drizzle with the vegetable oil and season with salt and pepper. Place the chops on the barbecue and cook to your liking; I cook for about 8–10 minutes for medium rare. When I cook meat on the barbecue I try to limit the amount of turns I make to get a good colour on the first side before flipping. That way you'll get nice grill lines on the meat. (Alternatively, cook the cutlets in a griddle pan over a high heat, turning once.)

5   Allow the cooked cutlets to rest for 5 minutes before arranging on a serving dish and smothering with the chermoula.

SALT AND PEPPER GRILLED QUAIL WITH CURRY LEAVES

You can prepare this dish inside during the colder months by using
a griddle pan to grill the quail or by pan-frying then roasting in the oven.
In summer, quails cook really well over coals and we particularly love
them this way. The magic is in the combination of flavours in the seasoning:
crisp curry leaves and coriander seeds. If you cannot find curry leaves,
don't worry; the dish will still be delicious without them. You could try
substituting some fried shallots from the Larder section (see page 288)
or even adding some toasted peanuts for a little crunch.

SERVES 6
100ml rapeseed oil
Small handful of curry
leaves (optional)
6 quail, ribcage and thighbones
removed (ask your butcher to do this)
50ml olive oil
Juice of ½ lemon
2 tbsp Sichuan Salt and Pepper
Seasoning (see page 286)

1   At least 30 minutes before you wish to cook, prepare your barbecue.
Light the coals and allow the flames to burn out and the coals to
achieve a consistent heat – the outer layer of the coal will be white
at this stage. Ensure the coals are evenly spread on the base of the
barbecue, leaving one corner without any coals. This empty portion
of the barbecue will offer a welcome escape area for any food
caramelising or burning too quickly.

2   Gently heat the rapeseed oil in a small pan over a medium heat.
Drop one curry leaf into the oil; if it sizzles, add some more.
Be careful not to add too many as the oil will sizzle up and could
overflow from the pan if too many are added too quickly.

3   Once all the leaves have been added and they are no longer sizzling,
remove the leaves from the pan and drain on kitchen paper to remove
excess oil. Set aside until needed.

4   Place the boned quail in a large bowl and dress with the olive oil.
Gently massage the oil onto the quail to ensure an even coating
on the skin. Be careful not to tear any limbs from the body at this
stage as they can be quite delicate.

5   Place each quail on the hot grill, skin side down, and leave for about
5 minutes to brown. You may have to move them around the grill
with a pair of tongs so they do not burn, depending on the temperature of the coals. Once they are golden and crispy on the skin side,
flip the birds over and cook for a further 3–4 minutes.

6   Place the cooked quail in a large clean bowl and squeeze over the
lemon juice. Sprinkle over the Sichuan seasoning and curry leaves
and stir well to coat the birds evenly in the seasoning. Pile the
birds up, one on top of another, and top with any remaining leaves,
seasoning and lemon juice from the bowl.

BABY BACK RIBS WITH GOCHUJANG KETCHUP

The perfect cooking time for ribs can be a tough thing to get just right. A rib that is overdone to the point that it yields no resistance at all can be as disappointing as one that sticks resolutely to the bone. When approaching the end of the braising process, check the ribs regularly. The meat should come away from the bone easily but not drop of as you lift the ribs from the master stock. The recipe below gives instructions for finishing in the oven, but these, like any ribs, love being finished on a barbecue, weather permitting. Let 'em burn!

SERVES 6
2kg baby back ribs
2 litres Master Stock (see page 287)
3 garlic cloves, smashed
40g fresh ginger, peeled and sliced
10 tbsp Gochujang Ketchup (see page 280)
Generous pinch of chilli flakes, to garnish
Handful of coriander leaves
8 lime wedges
Kimchi Slaw (see page 116), to serve

1   Preheat the oven to 170°C.

2   Place the ribs in a large roasting tray and pour over the stock. Add the garlic and ginger and top up with enough water to cover the ribs. Cover the tray with baking paper and then seal with foil.

3   Bake in the oven for 2–2½ hours, or until the meat is just coming away from the bone. Remove the tray from the oven, carefully lift the ribs from the stock and place on another large baking tray. Increase the oven temperature to 220°C.

4   Brush the gochujang ketchup evenly over both sides of the ribs and then return the ribs to the oven for 15 minutes, or until the sauce and ribs are beginning to caramelise. Alternatively, place over a hot barbecue (see page 208) and cook, turning often, for 5–10 minutes each side.

5   Remove from the oven, place on a chopping board and cut into manageable pieces. Sprinkle over the chilli flakes and coriander leaves and serve immediately with lime wedges and kimchi slaw on the side.

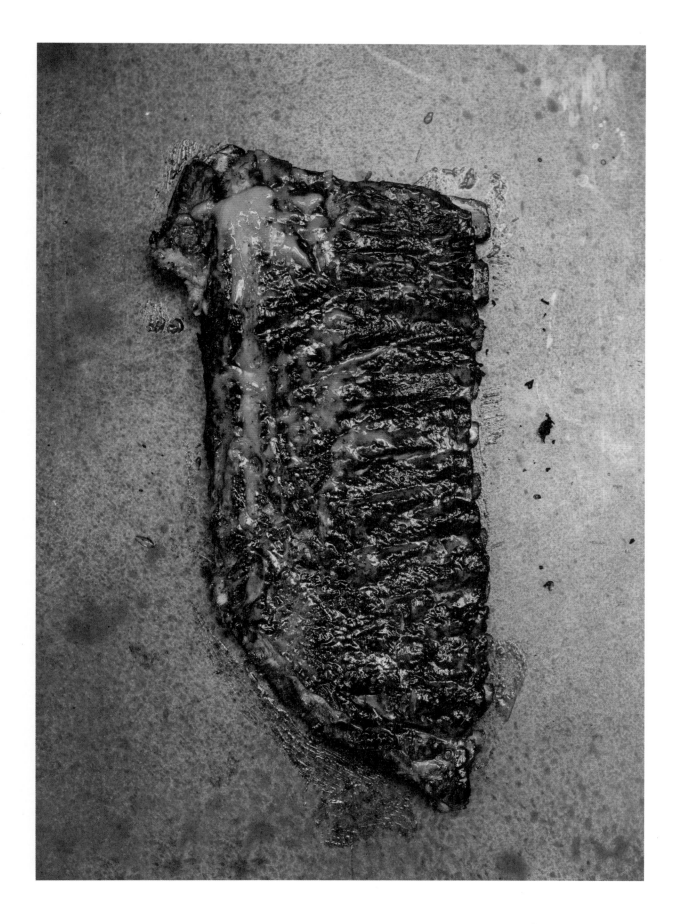

BRAISED RABBIT, SMOKED BACON, MUSTARD, CARROTS

Like chicken legs, rabbit legs like to be cooked slowly. The meat is similar to chicken, only a little sweeter and more prone to drying out when overcooked as it is so lean. The flavour is mild and it loves being cooked with things that bring more flavour to the party. Rabbit also loves a little bit of added fat, thus the streaky bacon and crème fraîche.

The timings in the recipe are for guidance only; you should check whether it is done at regular intervals throughout the cooking process.

SERVES 4–6
75ml rapeseed oil
6 wild rabbit legs and thighs
200g smoked streaky bacon, diced
100g shallots, diced
3 garlic cloves, sliced
100g leeks, sliced
10 thyme sprigs
4 medium carrots
300ml white wine
1.5 litres water
100g crème fraîche
20g Dijon mustard
Chopped flat-leaf parsley,
to garnish

1   Heat 50ml of the oil in a large, lidded casserole dish. Carefully place the rabbit into the hot oil and fry over a medium heat until they are brown on both sides. Do not overcrowd the pan with all the legs at once but rather do them in batches of 2 or 3 at a time. Once brown, remove from the pan and set aside on a tray or plate.

2   Add the smoked bacon to the pan and fry until browned, then remove from the pan and set aside with the rabbit.

3   Pour the remaining oil into the pan and, still over a medium heat, add the shallots, garlic, leeks and thyme. Fry until the vegetables are softened and starting to colour.

4   Place the whole carrots in the bottom of the pan and then add the white wine. Turn up the heat and reduce the wine by half. Return the bacon to the pan, place the rabbit on top of the carrots and then add the water. Bring to the boil, then reduce the heat and cover with a lid. Gently simmer for around 2½ hours, or until the meat feels tender but is still just clinging to the bone.

5   Remove the carrots and the rabbit from the pan and set them aside; keep warm in a tray covered with foil. Return the casserole to the heat and reduce the liquid over a high heat by two-thirds – this will probably take 25–30 minutes; in the last 5 minutes of cooking return the rabbit and the carrot to the casserole to heat through. Remove the pan from the heat and stir through the crème fraîche and the mustard. Scatter over the chopped parsley and serve.

BRAISED OXTAIL WITH ESPRESSO-RED WINE LIQUOR

A version of this dish was on our first menu at Caravan Exmouth Market. In the original version the idea was to braise in coffee. The coffee struggled to find its feet through the flavour of the oxtail. We now braise the oxtail without the coffee and add it later in the form of a red wine and espresso reduction: way better! We serve it with a creamy polenta (see the recipe for Shrimp 'n' Grits on page 76), which is a perfect base for juicy slow-cooked meats and sauces.

SERVES 6
Creamy polenta
(see page 76), to serve

GREEN SEASONING
Handful of coriander,
roughly chopped
1 celery stick, roughly chopped
3 garlic cloves, peeled
1 spring onion, chopped
3 tbsp fresh thyme leaves
Small handful of sage leaves,
roughly chopped
1 shallot
½ green chilli (or 1 small)

BRAISED OXTAIL
2kg oxtail, cut into 3–4cm pieces
(a butcher can do this for you)
30ml vegetable oil
4 tbsp muscovado sugar
2 large brown onions, sliced
4 small tomatoes, chopped
1 small leek, chopped
1 celery stick, chopped
4 garlic cloves, smashed
2 tbsp mustard seeds
3 bay leaves
1.2 litres water (enough to cover
the oxtail)
Sea salt and black pepper
Chopped flat-leaf parsley,
to garnish

ESPRESO AND RED WINE LIQUOR
300ml red wine
70g muscovado sugar
50g espresso coffee beans

1   First make the green seasoning. Combine all the ingredients in a food processor and blend to a paste. Set aside.

2   Trim off any excess fat from the oxtail and place in a large bowl. Massage the green seasoning into the oxtail and chill in the fridge for at least 2 hours, or overnight if possible.

3   When ready to cook the oxtail, preheat the oven to 180°C. Meanwhile, in a large heavy-based pan or casserole dish, heat the vegetable oil and the sugar and cook until the sugar starts to bubble. Ensure you keep the mixture moving and do not allow it to burn.

4   Working in batches so as not to overcrowd the pan, brown the oxtail pieces on all sides, transferring to a large bowl once each batch of oxtail is browned. Add the onions, tomatoes, leek, celery, garlic, mustard seeds and bay leaves to the pan and cook over a medium heat until the onion softens, stirring as you go.

5   Return the oxtail to the pan and cover with water. Bring to the boil, skim the foam off the top of the liquid, then cover with a lid and cook in the oven for 3–4 hours. The meat should be falling off the bone.

6   Meanwhile prepare the espresso-red wine liquor. Combine all the ingredients in a pan and bring to the boil. Simmer over a medium heat until the liquid has halved in volume, around 10 minutes. Pour into a container and cool. This will keep in the fridge for up to 2 weeks. Bring to room temperature before using and strain to remove the coffee beans.

7   About 10 minutes before you are ready to serve, prepare the polenta (see page 76).

8   Spoon the hot polenta onto a large sharing plate and spread out with the back of a spoon. Spoon the juicy oxtail over the polenta, including the yummy juice from the pan. Spoon over the room temperature liquor and sprinkle with chopped parsley. Season to taste with salt and pepper and serve with sautéed greens, cavolo nero or roasted heritage carrots.

SLOW-COOKED LAMB SHOULDER WITH BURNT GARLIC AND SHALLOTS

As we come from New Zealand, roasted lamb is never far from our minds. As a nation we eat our fair share of it and enjoy it for Christmas, at birthdays, Easter, Anzac Day, Labour Day and any occasion that calls for a celebration. It was always leg of lamb at our house – Mum thought that shoulder was too fatty for young children. It wasn't until I worked in restaurants that I uncovered the joys of slow-roasted shoulder of lamb. It needs a long cooking time to allow the meat to fall apart and some of the fat to melt. The caramelised garlic and shallots are just an added bonus.

I have known the Tilley family in North Wales for about 12 years now. I started buying their lamb after long conversations about whether New Zealand lamb or Welsh lamb is superior. I won't pass judgement on that just now as I love to chew the fat with Daphne on this subject. The truth is, Daphne represents a rare breed of wonderful farmer, who take the product literally from the farm to the front door of the restaurant, covering every base along the way.

This dish pairs really well with a simple leaf salad and saffron aioli (see pages 106 and 275) or with chermoula and a bulgur wheat salad (pages 208 and 100). (MK)

SERVES 6
1kg shallots, halved
250g garlic cloves, peeled but left whole
5 thyme sprigs
200ml water
1.6kg bone-in lamb shoulder
1 tbsp fine sea salt
1 tbsp cracked black pepper

1   Preheat the oven to 200°C.

2   Place the shallots and garlic cloves in the bottom of a high-sided roasting tray. Add the thyme sprigs and pour over 200ml water. Place the lamb shoulder on top and then season generously with the salt and pepper.

3   Cover the lamb with baking paper then seal the tray with aluminium foil. Place the lamb in the oven and cook for 30 minutes before turning the heat down to 160°C and leaving to cook for 4 hours.

4   Remove the foil and paper from the tray and again increase the heat to 200°C. Cook for a further 30–40 minutes, until the lamb is brown and has a delicious crisp layer on the outside.

5   Remove the lamb from the tray and set aside to rest, covered with foil to keep it warm. Strain any liquid from the roasting tray and then return the shallots and garlic to the oven. Continue to cook until they are burnt on top and sticking to the roasting dish, about 15–20 minutes. Scrape the burnt shallots and garlic from the tray and place in a sieve over a bowl to strain away any excess fat.

6   Using a pair of tongs or a couple of forks, tear large chunks of lamb from the bone and transfer to a serving plate. Spoon the burnt shallots and garlic onto the plate next to the lamb.

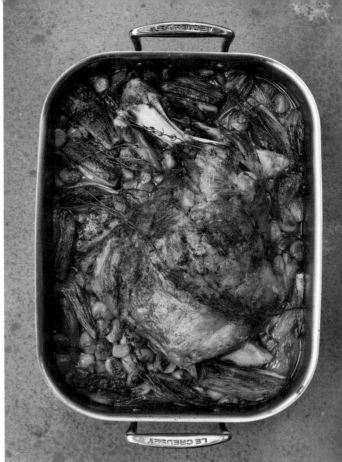

CHICKEN AND RICE

A staple on the staff meal rota in the early days at Caravan Exmouth Market, this dish was given a facelift after visiting Portland, Oregon, a couple of years ago and eating at the wonderful Nong's. Our experience in Portland elevated our basic staff meal of chicken and rice to a multi-layered feasting dish that is a total crowd-pleaser. At home we have it once a week for about 6 weeks until we get sick of it. Then the next time we have people for dinner it makes a comeback and stays on the menu for another 6 weeks again; it really is that good. The feast is made up of a number of elements that complement each other perfectly and are served as a help-yourself pick-and-mix. (MK)

SERVES 4
1 whole chicken, about 1.5kg
1 tbsp fine sea salt
5 coriander roots, bashed (or use coriander stalks and leaves)
50g fresh ginger, sliced
5 spring onions, chopped into 4 pieces
1 whole head of garlic, halved
1 tsp Sichuan peppercorns
3 star anise
1 cinnamon stick
1 lemongrass stick, bashed
1 onion, quartered
3 litres Chicken Stock (see page 287) or water
Fried Shallots (see page 288)

CHICKEN TEA
2 tbsp soy sauce
2 tbsp nam pla (fish sauce)
Handful of coriander (leaves and stalks)
10 Thai basil leaves
5g cassia bark or cinnamon
40g fresh ginger, peeled and sliced
1 tsp Sichuan peppercorns

SESAME CUCUMBER
1 cucumber
2 tbsp sesame oil
½ tsp fine sea salt
½ tsp black sesame seeds

1   Place the chicken in a large bowl and season inside and out with the sea salt. Stuff the coriander, ginger and spring onions inside the cavity of the chicken, then place into a large pan that has a tight-fitting lid.

2   Add the garlic, Sichuan pepper, star anise, cinnamon, lemongrass and onion to the pan then cover with chicken stock or water. Bring to the boil and then allow it to simmer for 25 minutes over a low heat. Cover with the lid, turn off the heat and allow the chicken to cool completely in the liquid.

3   Once cool, take the chicken out of the liquid and remove all the meat from the bone, retaining the skin from the bird. Slice the breast meat and pull the leg meat apart. Cover the chicken and set aside in the fridge until needed. Strain the liquid in the pan into a clean pan, reserving 500ml to cook the rice in later.

4   Now prepare the chicken tea. Bring the stock in the pan (you should have about 2 litres) back to the boil, add the soy sauce and the fish sauce then reduce the volume of the stock by a quarter. Set aside.

5   Place the coriander, Thai basil, cassia bark, ginger and Sichuan pepper into a teapot and set aside until ready to serve.

6   To make the crispy chicken skin, finely chop the reserved chicken skin and place into a cool non-stick frying pan. Gently heat the pan until the skin starts to sizzle. Maintain a gentle and consistent heat and stir as it fries to stop it from sticking to the pan. Continue to fry and stir for around 8–10 minutes until the skin is crispy and golden. Drain on kitchen paper and set aside until ready to use. (This needs to be used on the day it's made, as it will go chewy and stale with time.)

7   Slice the cucumber into thin rounds and place in a serving dish. Drizzle over the sesame oil and then sprinkle over the salt and black sesame seeds. Set aside.

YELLOW BEAN DRESSING
250ml white rice vinegar
175ml soy sauce
75ml yellow bean sauce
200ml filtered water
75ml sesame oil
50ml lime juice
100g caster sugar
15g fresh ginger, peeled and
very finely chopped

8 Combine all the ingredients for the yellow bean dressing in a
   bowl and stir to dissolve the sugar. Decant the sauce into a bottle
   or jar and store in the fridge for up to 2 weeks.

9 When you are nearly ready to serve, remove the poached chicken
   from the fridge to allow to come to room temperature. Wash the rice
   a couple of times in cold running water until the water runs clear.
   Drain well and then place the rice in a pan and cover with the 500ml
   reserved chicken stock. Place the pan over a high heat and bring
   to the boil. Boil for 2 minutes then place a lid on the pan and turn
   the heat off completely. Leave the rice with the lid on to cook for 15
   minutes via absorption method – do not lift the lid before this time.

10 Just before serving, bring the chicken tea back to the boil and pour
   it into the teapot over the aromatics. Place the pot on the table along
   with all the other elements and allow your guests to assemble their
   bowls as follows: cooked rice, poached chicken, cucumber, dressing,
   chilli oil, fresh coriander, fried shallots and crispy skin. Serve the
   tea in cups alongside the bowls.

PUDDING

We like to keep our puddings simple, rustic and unfussy at Caravan, both in preparation and in presentation. Actually, this approach is represented throughout all parts of our menu (give or take a few more intricate recipes for good measure), but we particularly relish a pudding that is simple, full of flavour and seasonal.

Most of the recipes in this section can be made in advance, making for a much more relaxed lunch, brunch or dinner party as you don't have to worry about preparing them while trying to entertain at the same time. We like things to be easy and uncomplicated at the end of a meal — a slice of tart, cake or cheesecake with a dollop of honey yoghurt or clotted cream can be a beautiful way to finish the proceedings.

VANILLA ICE CREAM WITH ESPRESSO AND SEA SALT CARAMEL

We have had a pop-up restaurant at the Frieze Art Fair in Regent's Park for the last 4 years. On the first year, we created this and it was so well received that this is now our go-to ice cream dessert in the restaurants. If you don't have an espresso machine at home, you can buy a couple of espresso shots and take them home for later use. You'll end up with enough caramel for about 10–15 servings but any unused sauce can be kept in an airtight container in the fridge for up to 8 days. To reuse, simply reheat gently in a pan.

MAKES 10–15 SERVINGS
50g muscovado sugar
50g caster sugar
50g golden syrup
50g unsalted butter
150ml double cream
50ml espresso
1 tsp flaked sea salt, plus extra to decorate (optional)
2 scoops of good-quality vanilla ice cream per person

1   Put both sugars, the golden syrup, butter and cream into a pan and gently heat and stir until the sugars have dissolved. Once melted, increase the heat to medium and simmer for 3 minutes, until the caramel becomes shiny and golden.

2   Remove from the heat and add the espresso and salt.

3   To serve, place 2 generous scoops of vanilla ice cream into small bowls or glasses and pour over the warm espresso caramel sauce. Top with a sprinkle of sea salt flakes, if using.

ROSE WATER BLANCMANGE WITH PISTACHIO PRALINE

Blancmange and rose water are two items that can cause a stir of negative emotion in the UK: blancmange conjures up images of a cold lumpy custard served for school dinners in days gone past, while rose water, when used excessively, can be reminiscent of pot pourri. However, when you combine the two in this simple recipe you are left with a delicious and refreshing summer pudding. A great friend of ours got married recently at Caravan King's Cross and her first and only real request was that we serve this dessert. It is delicious with the addition of fresh passion fruit or a fruit sorbet.

SERVES 4
500ml whole milk
150ml double cream
90g caster sugar
60g cornflour
100ml rose water
Dried edible rose petals,
to serve (optional)

PRALINE
150g pistachio nuts, toasted
in a dry pan
150g caster sugar
1 tbsp lemon juice

1   Place 450ml of the milk into a pan with the cream and sugar and bring to the boil. While you are waiting, combine the remaining 50ml milk and the cornflour in a small bowl to make a paste. As soon as the milk comes to the boil, whisk in the cornflour paste; the liquid will immediately thicken.

2   Reduce the heat to low and let the thickened mixture cook for a further minute, whisking all the time, then remove from the heat. Pass the mixture through a sieve into a large mixing bowl, stir in the rose water and set aside to cool to room temperature. Cover the surface of the blancmange directly with cling film to prevent a skin forming and chill in the fridge for 3 hours while you make the praline.

3   Preheat the oven to 160°C and line a baking tray with lightly oiled baking paper.

4   Spread the pistachio nuts on another baking tray in a single layer. Toast for 6–10 minutes until they are releasing nutty aromas. (Return to the oven briefly to warm through just before you add these to the caramel in the next step.)

5   In a pan, combine the sugar and lemon juice and place over a medium heat until the sugar caramelises and becomes an amber colour, swirling the pan rather than stirring. Use a wet pastry brush to brush the sides of the pan where sugar crystals may form. Add the hot nuts to the amber caramel and swirl until evenly covered. Pour the praline into the oiled, paper-lined tray in an even layer and allow to cool. Just before serving break the praline into pieces and roughly chop.

6   Remove the set blancmange from the fridge. You may want to check the consistency of the blancmange as it can vary depending on how long the milk/cream mixture initially took to heat up. If it seems too thick, add a little cold milk let it out. Simply whisk in the milk until you achieve the desired consistency. Pour the mixture evenly between 4 glasses or dessert bowls and decorate with the pistachio praline and rose petals (if using).

BLACK FIGS WITH GOAT'S CURD, BLOOD ORANGE MARMALADE AND PINE NUTS

This is a quick and simple pudding to prepare that relies on the figs being at their very best. If you can't find goat's curd then mixing a spoonful of honey through some Greek yoghurt will give great results too. For a dairy-free option, try coconut yoghurt.

SERVES 4
300g fresh goat's curd
Zest of 1 unwaxed lemon
80g Blood Orange Marmalade
(see page 273 or use shop-bought)
4 tablespoons water
6 ripe black figs
3 tbsp pine nuts, toasted
Torn mint leaves, to serve

1   Combine the goat's curd and the lemon zest in a large bowl and stir to combine the flavours. Allow to stand for 20 minutes before using.

2   Put the marmalade and water into a small pan and gently heat to make a wetter, more 'spoonable' marmalade sauce. (If you feel your marmalade is runny enough, you can skip this step.)

3   Spread the goat's curd over the base of a flat serving dish. Dollop three-quarters of the marmalade over the goat's curd in an uneven fashion, making lovely bright patches over the white curd.

4   Take each fig, remove the hard stalk and then tear each one in half. Place the figs in a mixing bowl and lightly dress with the remaining marmalade.

5   Spoon the dressed figs over the curd, making sure you spread them evenly over the curd. Sprinkle the pine nuts and torn mint over the top and serve.

COCONUT AND PANDAN FLAKED RICE PUDDING, BANANA CARAMEL, MANGO

Growing up, it often fell on my shoulders to make an impromptu pudding, mainly because I was the only one asking for pudding. My two sisters were professional dancers and generally speaking, pudding was off the menu.

My two go-to puddings were instant custard and – if we didn't have enough milk in the fridge – flaked rice pudding. These were both classics in eighties New Zealand and I really enjoyed developing this new and improved version when we opened Caravan. Adding an egg yolk at the end of the cooking process adds a great richness to the end product. Passion fruit is a good substitute for mango too, while toasted fresh coconut makes a great garnish. (MK)

SERVES 4–6
BANANA CARAMEL
100g caster sugar
1 tbsp lemon juice
1 banana, sliced

RICE PUDDING
200ml coconut milk
150ml whole milk
20g palm sugar or caster sugar
2 pandan leaves, chopped into large pieces (or use 2 vanilla pods, split and seeds scraped out)
75g flaked rice
1 large egg yolk
50ml double cream
1 mango, peeled and sliced

1 Place the sugar and lemon juice into a small pan and place over a medium heat. Use a wet pastry brush to brush the sides of the pan where sugar crystals may form and swirl the pan, rather than stir. Keep cooking until the sugar caramelises and turns an amber colour. Remove from the heat and allow it to cool. Once cool, add the sliced banana and stir. Set aside.

2 In a medium pan, heat the coconut milk, whole milk, sugar and pandan leaves or vanilla over a medium heat to infuse the flavour of the pandan into the liquid, about 10 minutes.

3 Strain to remove the pandan and return the liquid to pan, then bring to the boil and add the flaked rice. Reduce the heat and simmer for 3–5 minutes, stirring continuously, until the mixture thickens. Remove from the heat and stir though the egg yolk and double cream.

4 Evenly distribute between 4–6 small bowls or glasses. Spoon over the banana caramel, then top with sliced mango and serve.

PUMPKIN CHEESECAKE WITH PUMPKIN SEED PRALINE

This is a great recipe that works with butternut squash, pumpkin, sweet potato or most winter squash varieties. It is important that the flesh of the squash or pumpkin is firm and fresh and not stringy as this texture will carry through to the final product. The seed and nut base is a great wheat-free alternative to the usual biscuit crumbs and adds a great combination of earthy flavours and texture. As often happens with baked cheesecakes, you will sometimes get a crack in the top. Don't worry, we actually quite like the crack.

MAKES I CHEESECAKE
THE BASE
135g pumpkin seeds
135g pecans
35ml maple syrup
35g unsalted butter, melted
Pinch fine sea salt

FILLING
1kg butternut squash, peeled and deseeded
150g caster sugar
2 tbsp cornflour
500g cream cheese
1 medium egg
1 medium egg yolk
225g double cream
¼ tsp nutmeg

PUMPKIN SEED PRALINE
150g pumpkin seeds
150g caster sugar
1 tbsp lemon juice

1   First prepare the butternut squash for the filling. Preheat the oven to 180°C.

2   Cut the butternut squash into large chunks and tip onto a baking tray. Cover with foil and dry bake in the oven for 30–45 minutes, or until the squash is soft and cooked through. Remove from the oven and whizz in the food processor until you have a purée. Set aside to cool (you will need 450g purée for the cheesecake filling).

3   Reduce the oven temperature to 160°C and line a 24cm springform cake tin with baking paper.

4   In a food processer, whizz the pumpkin seeds and pecans for the base to a crumb-like mixture. Add the maple syrup, butter and salt and pulse until the mixture comes together and comes away from the sides of the food processor bowl. Press into the base of the prepared tin and bake for 18 minutes, then remove from the oven and set aside to cool while you make the rest of the filling.

5   In a stand mixer fitted with the paddle attachment, mix together the sugar, cornflour and cream cheese. Add the egg and egg yolk and mix to combine, then add the cream and nutmeg and mix on high speed until thick. Fold in 450g butternut purée by hand.

6   Pour the filling evenly on top of the cooked base and bake for 45 minutes – 1 hour until the mixture has a uniform wobble to it. Turn the oven off but leave the cheesecake in the oven for another hour, or until the oven has completely cooled. Remove from the oven and chill in the fridge overnight before serving.

7   To make the praline, preheat the oven to 160°C and line a baking tray with lightly oiled baking paper.

8   Spread the pumpkin seeds on another baking tray in a single layer. Toast for 6–10 minutes until they are releasing aromas. (Return to the oven briefly to warm through just before you add these to the caramel in the next step.)

9   In a pan, combine the sugar and lemon juice and place over a medium heat until the sugar caramelises and becomes an amber colour, swirling the pan rather than stirring. Use a wet pastry brush to brush the sides of the pan where sugar crystals may form. Add the hot pumpkin seeds to the amber caramel and swirl until evenly covered. Pour the praline into the oiled, paper-lined tray in an even layer and allow to cool.

10   Break the praline into small pieces and sprinkle over the top of the cheesecake to serve.

SEMOLINA CAKE WITH ROSEMARY SYRUP AND HONEY-YOGHURT CREAM

The end result here is a barely risen, dense-textured and extremely moist cake. Prick the cake with a bamboo skewer or fork a couple of times before pouring the syrup over the top – you may have to pour it in a couple of batches to allow the volume of syrup to be fully absorbed into the cake. If you flip the cake a couple of times during the syrup pouring phase, it will distribute the syrup a little more evenly without it sinking to the bottom.

MAKES I CAKE
300g caster sugar
360g yoghurt
2 tsp vanilla extract
290g coarse semolina
240g fine semolina
2 tsp baking powder
Zest of 4 unwaxed lemons
240ml whole milk
200g butter, melted

ROSEMARY SYRUP
400g unrefined golden caster sugar
540ml water
2 rosemary sprigs
2 tsp lemon juice

HONEY-YOGHURT CREAM
200ml double cream
200g Greek yoghurt
3 tbsp honey (we use New Zealand Manuka)

1   Preheat the oven to 175°C and butter and line a 22cm spring form cake tin with baking paper.

2   Combine the sugar, yoghurt and vanilla in a large bowl. Add the semolina, baking powder, lemon zest and milk and mix together.

3   Pour in the melted butter and allow to stand for 2 minutes to let the butter absorb. Mix until fully combined and then pour into the prepared cake tin. Bake for 45–50 minutes, or until a wooden skewer inserted into the middle comes out clean.

4   While the cake is baking, prepare the rosemary syrup and honey-yoghurt cream. Put all the ingredients for the syrup into a small pan and place over a low heat to dissolve the sugar and infuse the syrup with the flavour of the rosemary. Remove from the heat and allow to cool.

5   Whisk the cream to soft peaks, either with a hand-held electric whisk or using a stand mixer with the whisk attachment. Add the yoghurt and honey and gently mix. Chill in the fridge until ready to use.

6   As soon as the cake comes out of the oven, prick the surface with a skewer and pour the cooled syrup over the top of cake. Allow the cake to cool completely before removing the tin. Flip the cake over so it is bottom side up and serve in slices with a big dollop of honey-yoghurt cream. The cake will last for up to 5 days in the fridge.

CHERRY AND WALNUT TART

My natural instinct is to want to play around with ingredients and add something less expected to a recipe. Here, however, we have left things simple and classic as is often so good with puddings. The pastry is crisp and the frangipane is soft and moist and works in harmony with the tart juiciness of the cherries. Serve it with clotted cream. (MK)

MAKES 1 TART
300g fresh cherries, stones removed

SWEET PASTRY
175g plain flour
65g unsalted butter, chilled and diced
65g caster sugar
1 large egg
Pinch fine sea salt

WALNUT FRANGIPANE
100g walnuts
60g plain flour
200g unsalted butter, softened
200g caster sugar
3 medium eggs
1 medium egg yolk

1   Put the flour and butter into a stand mixer fitted with the paddle attachment to form a crumb-like texture. Add the sugar and mix again to combine. Add the egg and salt and paddle-mix very slowly until it comes together and away from the sides of the mixer. Tip onto a lightly floured work surface and form into a ball, then wrap in cling film and chill in the fridge for at least 45 minutes.

2   Roll the chilled pastry out on a floured work surface to a thickness of 4mm and large enough to line a 24cm fluted tart tin, about a 30cm circle. You may need to use more flour if the dough is sticky and a little too wet. Lay the rolled-out pastry into the tart tin and gently press the pastry into the sides of the tin. Leave any additional pastry hanging over the sides of the tin at this stage.

3   Prick the base of the pastry with a fork and then line with baking paper and fill with rice, dried chickpeas or ceramic baking beans. Place the raw tart shell back in the fridge to rest for a further 25 minutes. Preheat the oven to 180°C.

4   Blind bake the pastry case in the oven for 10–15 minutes, then remove the beans and paper and return to the oven for a further 10 minutes until the base is sandy to the touch but not too coloured. Set aside to cool while you make the frangipane but do not turn off the oven.

5   Place the walnuts and flour into a food processor and blend until you achieve a breadcrumb consistency. Cream the butter and sugar in a stand mixer fitted with the paddle attachment on medium speed until light and fluffy, about 5 minutes. Add the eggs and egg yolk one at a time, mixing well between each addition.

6   Fold the flour and the nuts into the mixture by hand, then spread the walnut frangipane evenly over the cooled pastry. Arrange two-thirds of the cherries on top and bake in the oven for 30 minutes until a crust forms on top of the tart. You will notice the cherries have mostly sunken into the tart and are no longer visible.

7   Carefully remove the tart from the oven and gently arrange the remaining cherries on top. Return to the oven and cook for a further 15–25 minutes, or until the tart is browned on top and there is no wobble left in the frangipane. Remove from the oven and set aside to cool. Once cool, carefully remove the tart from the tin and serve.

WARM CHOCOLATE PUDDINGS WITH CHOCOLATE SAUCE

This is a deliciously rich, warming pudding and will always be a favourite of ours. It is best served straight from the oven; the soft centre should explode onto the plate when cut open. We serve this in our restaurants with crème fraîche sorbet and lemon zest but good vanilla ice cream or a dollop of crème fraîche would work just as well.

MAKES 6
Cocoa powder, for dusting
120g unsalted butter
135g dark chocolate,
roughly chopped
3 medium eggs
2 medium egg yolks
100g caster sugar
55g plain flour, sifted

CHOCOLATE SAUCE
100g dark chocolate, chopped
150ml double cream

1   Preheat the oven to 180°C. Butter 6 × 220ml pudding dariole moulds or ramekins and dust the inside with cocoa powder, making sure you have a good coverage of cocoa.

2   Place the butter and chocolate in a heatproof bowl and set over a pan of barely simmering water, making sure the bottom of the bowl doesn't touch the water. Mix together until melted, then set aside.

3   In a stand mixer fitted with the whisk attachment, whisk the eggs, egg yolks and sugar on high speed until light and fluffy. Add the melted chocolate and butter mixture slowly, whisking on low speed as you pour it in. When all the ingredients have been combined, fold through the sifted flour by hand.

4   Evenly distribute the mixture between the 6 moulds. Place the moulds on a baking tray and bake in the oven for 12 minutes.

5   Meanwhile make the chocolate sauce. Put the cream into a pan and place over a medium-low heat (do not let the cream boil). Add the chocolate and stir/swirl over a low heat until the chocolate has melted.

6   Remove the cooked puddings from the oven and allow to cool a little before turning out onto plates. Pour the sauce over the top and serve with crème fraîche, yoghurt or vanilla ice cream.

We love a drink at Caravan and so do a lot of our friends and customers, so creating our cocktail, wine and brunch drinks lists over the years has always been a hugely pleasurable and often elongated process. If it's not coffee we are serving, we are equally passionate about providing the right lubricant for the right time of day.

When we wrote our first cocktail menu, we had a penchant for the classics, which has now given way to classics with a twist, as well as some that are totally unique and as unusual as possible. Our bar team is constantly playing around with tinctures and shrubs, barrel ageing, fat washing, fermenting, steeping, infusing and dehydrating all manner of ingredients and creations, which we wholeheartedly encourage. We have included three Caravan twists on a classic here, but only because we wanted to keep things simple, delicious and easy to prepare.

For breakfast and brunch, we evolve our freshly pressed juices, shots and smoothies with the seasons. Perfect for starting the day and super easy to make, we often make a large juice or smoothie batch before guests arrive to serve before or with brunch. But of course, if your brunch feast requires a more robust tipple, our bloody Mary or breakfast martini will not disappoint and will definitely keep the party going.

Our wine lists have always been well travelled and internationally inspired. In creating these lists, we have sought out emerging wine-making regions, uncommon grape varieties or vineyards growing grapes not usually grown in that region. We have also championed the increasing trend for natural, organic or biodynamic wines and list as many of these as possible, provided always that they taste great.

GINGER, LEMON AND CAYENNE SHOT

Seriously intense in flavour and punch, this shot is a great way to start the day. Add as little or as much cayenne as you can handle!

MAKES 4
4 thumb-sized pieces of ginger
1 large lemon (peeled)
Pinch cayenne pepper

1   Using a counter-top electric juicer, juice the lemon and ginger. Combine thoroughly and add a small pinch of cayenne pepper (a larger pinch is not for the faint hearted!). Taste and add more cayenne if needed. Pour equally between 4 shot glasses and serve.

WHEATGRASS, SMOKED JALAPEÑO, CORIANDER AND LIME SHOT

Mini shots with concentrated goodness are a great way to start the day or to give you a little pick-me-up in the afternoon and – dare we say it – this juice base would also make a killer vodka cocktail too. Play around with the ratio and type of jalapeño, depending on how punchy you like your flavours to be. If you are looking for something really spicy and fresh, go for fresh jalapeños, although tinned jalapeños, smoked or plain, also work really well.

MAKES 4 SHOTS
2 jalapeño chillies, fresh or tinned
Large handful of coriander leaves and stalks
¾ large cucumber, cut into
3 large chunks
15ml freshly squeezed lime juice
80ml filtered water
2 tsp wheatgrass powder

1   Feed the jalapeños, coriander and cucumber through a juicer into a jug. Add the fresh lime juice and stir to combine

2   Place the water into another jug or glass and stir in the wheatgrass powder, making sure that you stir well to combine and release any grittiness of the wheatgrass. Add to the jalapeño, coriander and cucumber juice and stir well.

3   Pour into four shot or mini glasses and drink quickly for an instant pick-me-up.

CARROT, APPLE, GINGER AND FRESH TURMERIC JUICE

This is a real classic and a juice that we serve vast quantities of throughout the week. If you don't have turmeric root to hand, you can always add a teaspoon of ground turmeric at the end and stir through. Don't be tempted to leave it out: turmeric has anti-inflammatory and antioxidant qualities and adds a great depth of colour to the juice as well.

SERVES I
3 carrots, washed, topped
and tailed
2 crisp Braeburn apples, quartered
if necessary to fit through
your juicer
Thumb-sized piece of fresh
ginger, washed
10g fresh turmeric root, washed
3 ice cubes

1   Feed the carrots, apples, ginger and turmeric root through the feeder tube of your juicer.

2   Pour into a highball glass over the ice.

SPINACH, APPLE, PARSLEY, LEMON AND CUCUMBER JUICE

We have been serving this juice at our restaurants for a number of years now; every time it comes off the menu, we get so many requests to put it back on that we invariably give in to pressure. It is such a fresh, clean, healthy juice that is full of goodness and delicious at any time of the year. It will likely still be on the drinks menu in years to come.

SERVES I
Large handful of baby
spinach leaves
2 Granny Smith apples, quartered
if necessary to fit through
your juicer
Large handful of flat-leaf parsley
leaves and stalks
10 mint leaves
½ cucumber, skin on
2 tsp fresh lemon juice
3 ice cubes

1   Feed the spinach, apples, parsley, mint and cucumber through the feeder tube of your juicer. Depending on what type of juicer you have, it can be helpful to roll the parsley and mint around the cucumber to ensure it extracts properly.

2   Pour the green goodness into a highball glass over the ice, add the lemon juice and stir to combine.

KALE, AVOCADO, NUT BUTTER, ALMOND MILK SMOOTHIE

Chris, Miles and I started going to the gym together on a Wednesday morning before our weekly director meetings, the theory being that our minds would be raring to go after a good workout. We created this smoothie to give our bodies a boost after our training session and to hopefully see us through the inevitable drudgery of discussing financials, lease renewals and operations. There are lots of good organic nut butters available these days, so feel free to experiment with your favourite – see our Almond Butter recipe on page 272, or look out for pure peanut butter. (LHH)

SERVES 2
½ avocado, peeled and stone removed
½ banana
Small handful of kale leaves, washed
1 tbsp cashew butter or Almond Butter (see page 272 or use shop-bought)
1 tsp raw honey
300ml unsweetened almond milk
3 ice cubes
Squeeze of lime or lemon juice (optional)

1   Place all the ingredients except the lime or lemon juice in a high-speed blender or smoothie maker and blitz until well combined, or until you have a thick, smooth, liquid consistency. If you like your smoothies to have a bit more acidity, add a squeeze of lime or lemon and stir through at the end after you have tasted it.

2   Pour into highball glasses, drink and feel energised.

CACAO, ALMOND, BANANA, TAMARIND AND DATE SMOOTHIE

We love the balance of sweet, sour, creamy and bitter in this drink. Combining lots of good stuff, it is the perfect start to the day or for after the gym (add some hemp protein powder for an extra boost). It makes a great weekend brunch as kids will love this smoothie as much as adults.

SERVES 1
1 tsp cacao nibs, plus extra for sprinkling
1 tsp Tamarind and Date Purée (see page 42)
2 pitted Medjool dates
½ banana
300ml unsweetened almond milk
2 ice cubes

1   Place all the ingredients in a blender and blitz on high speed to ensure the cacao nibs and dates break down.

2   Pour into a highball glass, sprinkle on some extra cacao nibs if you like and enjoy.

SALTED CARAMEL HOT CHOCOLATE

We created this for our opening at Caravan King's Cross and it has been a great addition to the menu. It is warming, soothing, sweet, salty and rich all at the same time and would be a great thing to make for afternoon 'tea' on a cold winter's day. You need to make the chocolate ganache and salted caramel at the same time so that you can combine them while still warm. This mixture will then keep in the fridge for up to 5 days, so you can make it ahead of time and then all you have to do is warm the milk when you fancy a delicious warming hot chocolate.

MAKES 10 SERVINGS
125ml warm milk per serving

CHOCOLATE GANACHE
140ml double cream
45ml water
45g caster sugar
130g dark (at least 60% cocoa solids) chocolate chunks or buttons

SALTED CARAMEL
50g caster sugar
10ml water
80ml double cream
¼ tsp flaked sea salt

1   First make the chocolate ganache. Combine the cream, water and sugar in a medium pan and place over a medium-low heat to dissolve the sugar. Do not let it come to the boil but remove from the heat just before it does. Place the dark chocolate in a heatproof bowl, pour the hot liquid over it and stir until the chocolate melts.

2   Meanwhile make the salted caramel by combining the sugar and water in a small pan and heating gently to make a dark amber caramel (see page 168). Remove the caramel from the heat and allow it to cool for 5 minutes, then slowly add the cream and salt. Return the pan to the heat and bring the caramel back to the boil.

3   Remove from the heat and combine with the chocolate ganache while still warm. If not using straight away, allow to cool and then store in an airtight container in the fridge.

4   To make a hot chocolate, put 50ml of the salted caramel chocolate ganache into the bottom of a mug or thick-walled glass. Slowly pour warmed milk over the ganache until the glass is half full and stir to combine. Top with the remaining milk and serve.

BREAKFAST MARTINI

When we first opened Caravan Exmouth Market, we decided that this would be the first brunch cocktail on our menu. It is such a great way to kick-start a boozy, long brunch and it is unlikely we will take it off our menu anytime soon. We serve our breakfast martinis with a slice of sourdough toast and marmalade to keep it real. We are not suggesting you start every brunch session this way, but it is certainly fun sometimes.

SERVES 1
50ml London Dry-style gin
25ml sweet red vermouth
20ml fresh pressed orange juice
2tsp orange marmalade or Blood
Orange Marmalade (see page 273
or use shop-bought)
Ice cubes

1   Combine the gin, vermouth, orange juice and marmalade in a cocktail shaker. Stir the contents of the shaker well to break down the marmalade then fill the smaller part of the shaker with ice and shake hard for 10 seconds.

2   Pour through a strainer into a pre-chilled martini glass.

3   Serve with toast and marmalade.

FERMENTED CHILLI AND SMASHED CUCUMBER BLOODY MARY

We created this Bloody Mary for the first pop-up restaurant we did at the Frieze Art Fair 4 years ago. If you like things really spicy, try upping the gochujang (Korean fermented bean paste with chilli), though the Sichuan chilli oil in the smashed cucumbers will give an extra hit too.

SERVES 1
1 tsp gochujang
200ml fresh tomato juice
Pinch salt and pepper
50ml wheat-based vodka
Ice
3–4 pieces Smashed Cucumber
(see page 122)
Freshly cracked black pepper,
to garnish

1   In a shaking tin, combine the gochujang, tomato juice and salt and pepper.

2   Muddle the ingredients using a muddler or wooden spoon to combine, add the vodka, and stir well.

3   Pour the mixture into a highball glass with 4–5 cubes of ice and garnish with a few pieces of smashed cucumber and some cracked pepper.

CARAVAN CLASSIC BLOODY MARY

No brunch would be complete without a delicious Bloody Mary to go with it. We have been making this version for years and it never fails to satisfy as it has a good depth of flavour and a spicy kick. We like to have a good amount of the Bloody Mary essence ready to go for big brunch sessions with family and friends. Even the kids like a little bit of the essence with lots of plain tomato juice.

SERVES 1
50ml wheat-based vodka
50ml Bloody Mary essence
125ml fresh tomato juice
Ice
1 celery stick
1 lemon wedge
Freshly cracked black pepper

BLOODY MARY ESSENCE
(MAKES 10 PORTIONS)
300ml tomato juice
75ml Worcestershire sauce
2 tbsp Dijon mustard
2 tsp grated horseradish
10ml Tabasco sauce
Handful of coriander, chopped
Pinch each of salt and black pepper

1   First make the Bloody Mary essence. Combine all the ingredients in a blender and blitz for 30 seconds. This will keep in the fridge for up to 5 days.

2   Combine the vodka, Bloody Mary essence and tomato juice in a highball glass and stir to combine all the ingredients.

3   Top with ice and garnish with celery, a lemon wedge and cracked black pepper.

CHEF'S MARGARITA

We are always trying to encourage as much 'cross-pollination' between our kitchen, bar and front-of-house teams as possible. This leads to better relationships between the teams and hopefully some great creativity along the way. The bar and kitchen teams at our King's Cross restaurant created this margarita together and it really is a harmonious combination. When blood oranges are not in season, any other type of orange will do, but you won't get the same beautiful bright red hue.

MAKES 1
50ml reposado tequila
15ml triple sec
15ml lime juice
15ml blood orange juice
Lime wedge

SMOKED CUMIN SEA SALT
1 tsp cumin seeds
Zest of 1 lime
Zest of 1 unwaxed lemon
Zest of 1 unwaxed orange
2 tbsp smoked sea salt

1   First prepare the smoked cumin sea salt. Place a non-stick frying pan over a low heat. Add the cumin seeds to the pan and allow them to toast for 2–3 minutes until they start to turn brown and release their aroma. Tip the seeds into a mortar.

2   Add the grated citrus zests to the warm pan and put to one side while it cools down. During this time, the zest should dry out. If it doesn't fully dry, place the pan in a warm place until the zest dries completely. Add the dried zests to the cumin seeds and pound gently to break up all the seeds (you are not looking for a powder). Finally, add the salt to the mixture and stir to combine.

3   In a cocktail shaker, combine the tequila, triple sec, lime juice and orange juice. Run the wedge of lime around the rim of a chilled rocks or saucer martini glass then then dip the rim into the smoked cumin salt.

4   Add ice to the shaker and shake furiously for 10 seconds. Strain the drink into the salt-rimmed glass and enjoy.

NOTE

This smoked cumin salt also makes a great alternative seasoning for sweetcorn (see page 138), or use to season grilled lamb chops instead of chermoula (see page 208).

ESPRESSO MARTINI

Well we could hardly call ourselves a coffee roaster, restaurant and bar without having one of these on the menu, could we? We have tweaked and changed the recipe over the years and at the restaurants we use our own house-made coffee bitters. We have simplified the recipe to make athome, but the results are no less satisfying. If you do not have an espresso machine at home, get a couple of shots of espresso from your local specialty coffee shop.

MAKES 1
30ml good-quality vodka
15ml coffee liqueur, such as Kahlua
10ml sugar syrup (see Note)
50ml shot of espresso
Ice

1 Combine the vodka, coffee liqueur and sugar syrup in a cocktail shaker, before adding the shot of espresso last.

2 Fill the shaker with ice and place the lid on, making sure it is on securely. Shake up a storm for about 10 seconds, holding the shaker firmly. The longer you shake for, the more crema foam you will get at the top of the drink – you will also get a bit more volume in the glass.

3 Strain the drink into a pre-chilled glass of your choice and serve.

NOTE

You can make a simple sugar syrup for cocktails by gently heating 1 part unrefined golden caster sugar with 1 part water until the sugar has dissolved (do not boil). Remove from the heat and allow to cool before using – it will keep for several weeks in the fridge.

COFFEE NEGRONI

The Negroni is one of our all-time favourite cocktails, so adding a delicious single-origin coffee syrup to the mix seemed like great idea. We created this for the London Coffee Festival a few years back and it went down a treat; it has become a staple on our bar menus ever since. It's key to source a good-quality, specialty coffee by a local roaster to use for your single-origin filter. You want a clean, full-flavoured coffee without any bitterness – leave that to the Campari!

MAKES 1

25ml London Dry-style gin
25ml Campari
25ml single-origin coffee
syrup, chilled
Ice
Twist of orange peel

COFFEE SYRUP

250ml single-origin filter coffee
50g unrefined golden caster sugar

1   First make the coffee syrup. Make 250ml single-origin filter coffee using a Chemex, V60, Aeropress or your favourite home filter coffee. Add the unrefined caster sugar and stir to dissolve. Allow the syrup to cool fully before using and store in an airtight container in the fridge for up to 7 days (you will have enough for about 10 cocktails).

2   In a chilled tumbler, combine the gin, Campari and coffee syrup. Fill the glass with ice and stir for 5–10 seconds to combine the ingredients. Garnish with a thick twist of orange peel, squeezing to release the oils all over the glass.

LARDER

Every kitchen has its own unique and original flavour DNA and at the heart of this is the kitchen larder. Caravan is no exception and there are certain spice and herb combinations, sauces, pickles, dressings and vinegars that keep our kitchens ticking over and that we couldn't live without. We always have these items on hand or in the fridge as our go-to seasonings when building a dish. From there, we encourage our chefs to explore and go on their own culinary journey to create simple, full-flavoured creations.

The thing we love the most about our kitchen larder at Caravan is that thanks to our well-travelled food concept, which is not restricted by culinary boundaries, our larder spans countries and continents and so the options for flavour combinations are unlimited. We remain rooted to local, seasonal, sustainable produce wherever possible, but the added flavours that make our dishes special are definitely an international affair.

The larder recipes we have included have stood the test of time in our kitchen and represent some of the important flavours that resonate through our food. You will soon find yourselves turning to these on a regular basis and wonder how you lived without them.

RYE LAVASH

These crisp Middle Eastern flatbreads are a staple in our kitchens. They are great served with cheese and chutney. They are an excellent bread to serve with hummus but perhaps our favourite use is broken up, and served with a roasted vegetable or green leaf salad to add that sometimes needed crunch.

SERVES 6 (WITH CHEESE)
100g rye flour
½ tsp caster sugar
½ tsp sea salt
1 tsp olive oil, plus extra for brushing
120ml cold water
Flaked sea salt, to sprinkle
Sesame and nigella seeds, to sprinkle

1   Mix the dry ingredients together in a medium bowl. Stir in the olive oil and water and massage together until a smooth ball is formed, around the size of a tennis ball. Wrap the ball in cling film and rest in the fridge for at least 1 hour, preferably overnight.

2   Preheat the oven to 180°C and line a baking tray with baking paper.

3   Remove the dough from the fridge, unwrap and then gently roll on a lightly floured work surface to a thickness of 1mm. You may need to dust the surface of the dough with flour as you roll. Place on the baking tray and prick the surface all over with a fork. Bake for 12–15 minutes until firm and golden.

4   Remove from the oven, brush with olive oil and sprinkle with salt and sesame and nigella seeds. Allow to cool then snap into manageable-sized pieces and store in an airtight container until ready to use. The lavash will keep for 3–5 days, but is best used fresh.

BUCKWHEAT LAVASH

70g buckwheat flour
65g plain flour
¼ tsp fine sea salt
1 tsp olive oil
80ml cold water
Flaked sea salt, to sprinkle
Nigella seeds, to sprinkle

1   Make, rest, roll and bake exactly as for the Rye Lavash, left.

ALMOND BUTTER

There are an increasing number of good-quality shop-bought nut butters available these days, but there is no substitute for making your own, especially as it is so easy to do. We use almond and cashew butters in our smoothies, in our baked goods and on bread instead of peanut butter. It is a great thing to have on hand.

MAKES ABOUT 400g
250g whole blanched almonds
150ml vegetable oil
1 tsp fine sea salt

1   Preheat the oven to 170°C.

2   Place the almonds in a baking tray, pour the oil over and roast in the oven for 10–12 minutes until golden. Remove the tray from the oven and allow to cool.

3   Once nearly cool, place the almonds, oil and salt in a food processor and blitz until completely smooth. If the mixture is not blitzing to a paste, add a little more oil to loosen the mixture up.

4   Store in an airtight container in the fridge for up to 2 weeks.

BLOOD ORANGE MARMALADE

This super-easy recipe makes for a deliciously bitter marmalade that is great with a slice of buttered sourdough and a breakfast martini. Using powdered pectin rather than relying on the natural pectin in the seeds will create a more consistent result, so we have included it here. If you want, you can try collecting the seeds, wrapping them in a muslin cloth and adding them to the pan at the first stage. The natural pectin in the seeds will help the marmalade set.

MAKES I LARGE JAR
12 blood oranges
800g caster sugar
250ml blood orange juice
50ml lemon juice
2 star anise
1 cinnamon stick
3 tbsp pectin powder
100ml water

1   Sterilise a 2-litre Kilner jar by scrubbing well and then rinsing with boiling water. (Alternatively you can use straight from the dishwasher.)

2   Cut the blood oranges in half and then slice each half into 6 half-moon slices, around 2mm thick. Remove any seeds and place the orange slices into a large stainless steel pan.

3   Add the sugar, orange and lemon juice, star anise and cinnamon to the pan and bring to the boil over a high heat. Reduce the temperature and cook at a simmer for 20–25 minutes until the sugar has turned to a shiny syrup. Meanwhile dissolve the pectin in the water and set aside.

4   Increase the heat and bring back to a boil. Stir in the pectin and boil for 5 minutes. Turn off the heat and leave in the pan to cool down slightly.

5   When the jam is cool enough to handle, pour into the sterilised jar and seal. Once opened it will keep for up to 3 weeks.

MAYONNAISE

I am a firm believer that most things taste better with mayonnaise. It is a guilty pleasure of mine but not one I spend much time worrying about. Make sure the eggs you are using are super-fresh and always free-range and organic.

If your stand mixer is anything like mine, it prob-ably won't whisk one egg yolk very efficiently, but rather whisk the air just above the egg. I either double the recipe quantities or whisk by hand. I recommend making mayonnaise by hand at least once, as it will give you a real sense and understanding of the emulsification that takes place. My only other recommendation is, of course, that you put this mayo, either in its classic form or as one of the variations given overleaf, on everything. (MK)

MAKES 250ml
1 egg yolk
1 tsp Dijon mustard
1 tbsp apple cider vinegar
¼ tsp fine sea salt
250ml vegetable oil or other neutral-flavoured oil
1 tbsp warm water

1   In a stand mixer fitted with the whisk attachment, whisk together the yolk, mustard, vinegar and salt on medium speed until pale in colour and a thick consistency.

2   With the mixer still on medium speed, very slowly pour in the oil until it begins to emulsify, at which point you can speed up the pouring.

3   As you pour in the oil, you may notice the mixture thickening so that it no longer binds together. At this point, add the warm water to loosen the mixture.

4   Continue to pour the rest of the oil slowly on medium speed to combine. You should end up with lovely balanced, thick mayonnaise.

5   Store in the fridge in an airtight container for up to 3 days.

CITRUS MAYONNAISE

My favourite use for this mayo is with deep-fried oysters (see page 176). It is also great with smoked fish, particularly mackerel. A dollop in a bowl of grainy vegetable soup will lift it to new levels of deliciousness. (MK)

1 quantity of Mayonnaise (see previous page)
Zest of 2 unwaxed lemons
2 tbsp lemon juice
Zest of 2 limes
1 tbsp lime juice
½ tsp cracked black pepper

1   Place the mayonnaise in a bowl and mix with the lemon zest and juice and lime zest and juice. Season with freshly cracked pepper to taste.

AIOLI

For a punchier aioli, you can grate in 1 small raw garlic clove but be careful not to overdo it though. Another great addition is wild garlic, when it's in season. Blanch the leaves and blend or mash to a purée. Stir through the mayonnaise to achieve a great green sauce.

1 quantity of Mayonnaise (see previous page)
100g Confit Garlic (see page 276)

1   Combine the mayonnaise and confit garlic and whisk well to combine.

2   Store in an airtight container in the fridge for up to 3 days.

SAFFRON AIOLI

Another Caravan go-to condiment that has had plenty of use over the years. Prawns, croquettes, squash and grilled aubergine salads love it.

1 tsp good-quality saffron threads
3 tbsp water
1 quantity of Aioli (see above)

1   Put the saffron and water into a small pan and heat gently to infuse the water with the saffron flavour. Set aside to cool.

2   Pour the cooled saffron water, including the threads, into the aioli and stir through.

3   Store in an airtight container in the fridge for up to 3 days.

CONFIT GARLIC

Confit garlic can be used for many things and provides an excellent alternative to raw garlic as it has a softer, less astringent garlicky flavour. In cooking the cloves, the flavour softens and becomes less intense; the profile changes to a sweet and delicate morsel that is a great addition to any dish that asks for garlic. We highly recommend that you keep a jar of these in your fridge at all times. It's so easy to make and keeps well if covered with oil.

MAKES ABOUT 250g
275g garlic cloves, peeled (about 4 whole bulbs)
300ml olive oil
3 thyme sprigs

1   Place all the ingredients in a small pan, place over a high heat and bring to the boil.

2   Turn the heat down to low and simmer for 20–25 minutes until the cloves are soft – the garlic should be a little brown at the edges, but not browned all over.

3   Turn the heat off and allow it to cool. This will keep in an airtight container in the fridge for up to 6 weeks.

MISO-SESAME DRESSING

Atari goma is sesame paste from Japan and comes in a white or black sesame version. If you cannot get to a Japanese food store, just use tahini, which you can find anywhere. The results are similar but you may have to let the dressing out with a little more water. We use this dressing for grain bowls, with cold soba noodles or drizzled over roasted vegetables; it goes particularly well with squash, parsnips and spring greens.

MAKES ABOUT 250ml
4 tbsp shiro miso paste
4 tbsp atari goma (or use tahini)
4 tbsp honey
4 tbsp cold water
2 tbsp pickled ginger purée
2 garlic cloves, finely grated

1   Combine all the ingredients in a medium bowl and whisk well to combine.

2   Store in an airtight container in the fridge for up to 10 days.

BASIC SOY PICKLE

This simple three-part marinade or pickle juice is great for pickling cucumber and daikon. Equally it makes a great base for a dressing and loves being enhanced with garlic and ginger. If using for a dressing, try letting it out with a little olive oil and/or truffle oil. It is also delicious with raw scallops and as a dressing for raw oysters.

MAKES 300ml
100ml mirin
100ml light soy sauce
100ml rice wine vinegar
15g ginger, finely chopped
1 garlic clove, halved

1   Combine all the ingredients in a small bowl. Allow to stand for 30 minutes and then strain to remove the garlic and ginger.

2   This will keep in the fridge in an airtight container for several weeks.

ONION-SHRIMP CHILLI JAM

There is always a jar of this oniony chilli jam in our fridge. It is great with a piece of fried fish and equally delicious served as an extra condiment with roast chicken. My favourite use is at breakfast time, served on top of toasted sourdough bread smothered with cream cheese. It's a little wrong but very right. (MK)

MAKES ABOUT 2 CUPS
100g garlic cloves, peeled
75g fresh ginger, peeled and roughly chopped
110g palm sugar, grated
40g dried shrimp, toasted
150g tamarind water or paste
150ml rapeseed oil or other neutral-flavoured oil
1kg (about 4 large) red onions, halved and sliced
200g (about 8 large) red chillies, sliced
220ml nam pla (fish sauce)

1   Place the garlic and ginger in a food processer and blitz until even blended. Transfer to a bowl and set aside.

2   Place the palm sugar, dried shrimp and tamarind into the food processor and process until smooth. Transfer to a separate bowl and set aside.

3   Heat the oil in a medium pan, add the onions and cook over a medium heat until soft, around 10 minutes.

4   Add the sliced chillies and blended garlic and ginger and cook for a further 10 minutes. Now add the palm sugar, shrimp and tamarind mixture and cook over a low heat for about 1 hour, stirring occasionally, until a dark caramelised colour. When you stir it, it should stick together in a ball. Turn off the heat and allow to cool in the pan.

5   Store the jam in sterilised jars (see page 273) in the fridge for up to a month.

HARISSA

There are many ways to make harissa, but this version is our favourite. It's really versatile – we always have a batch in the fridge at home and it's on our menus in one shape or form pretty much all the time. Use it on chargrilled meats and vegetables, with yoghurt as a dressing for grains or (our current favourite) as the base for a pizza with sprouting broccoli and mozzarella.

MAKES ABOUT 1½ CUPS

1 red pepper
25g dried chipotle chilli
25g dried ancho chilli
1 tsp caraway seeds
1 tsp coriander seeds
1 tsp cumin seeds
4 garlic cloves, smashed

80ml lemon juice
1 tsp fine sea salt
1 tsp tomato purée
Handful of coriander leaves
Small handful of mint leaves
½ tsp smoked paprika
80ml extra-virgin olive oil

1   Place the red pepper directly on the gas flame of your hob and turn the heat up. Using a pair of tongs, regularly turn the pepper over and around to burn the skin on all sides. The skin should be blistered and black all over.

2   Place the blistered pepper in a bowl and cover it tightly with cling film. Set aside to cool. Once cool, peel off the burnt skin, discard any seeds and excess juice and place in a high-speed blender or liquidiser (at home I use a high-speed smoothie maker).

3   Place the dried chillies in another bowl and cover with boiling water to rehydrate them. Set aside. Once they are cool and fully rehydrated, drain off the liquid, remove the hard stalks and the seeds and then place the chillies in the blender with the charred pepper.

4   In a heavy-based frying pan, toast the caraway, coriander and cumin seeds over a low heat until they are a light brown toasted colour and they smell toasted and sweet. Transfer the toasted seeds to a mortar and grind to a fine powder with a pestle. Tip the ground spices into the blender with the pepper and chillies. Add all the remaining ingredients and blitz on high speed to a fine paste.

5   Transfer to an airtight container and store in the fridge for up to a week.

KOREAN PEPPER 'HARISSA'

This recipe came about initially as a by-product from making kimchi. It's really easy to make and is a great condiment for fish and chicken particularly. It is also great stirred through a wok of Chinese greens.

MAKES ABOUT 1½ CUPS

5 tbsp gochugaru (red pepper flakes)
2 garlic cloves, chopped
Thumb-sized piece of fresh ginger, peeled and chopped
½ large onion, chopped
Bunch of coriander stalks
1 tbsp caster sugar
5 tbsp nam pla (fish sauce)
5 tbsp rice wine vinegar
2 tbsp lime juice
5 tbsp rapeseed oil

1   Place the red pepper flakes, garlic, ginger, onion, coriander stalks and sugar into a food processor and blend until you have a fine salsa-like consistency.

2   Add the fish sauce, vinegar and lime juice and blend again to combine. Finally add the oil and pulse to combine.

3   Store in an airtight container in the fridge for up to 3 days.

GREEN CHILLI ZHOUG

Zhoug is one of our favourite sauces – simple, yet seriously full of flavour and punch. Originating from Yemen, it is also a popular relish in Israel and likely many other Middle Eastern countries. If you can find them, use green serrano peppers for this recipe as they are sweet and have a great kick (and this sauce is supposed to be hot). Otherwise regular green chillies also work, although if you want to add some serious heat, add in a bird's eye chilli (or scud chilli, as we call them in our kitchens). Drizzle over anything when you want to add some kick!

MAKES ABOUT ½ CUP
65g coriander, leaves and stalks chopped
130g green chillies, deseeded and chopped
1½ tsp fine sea salt
1 garlic clove, very finely chopped
200ml rapeseed oil
1½ tbsp lemon juice

1   Place the coriander, chilli, salt and garlic in a food processor and blend to paste. Transfer to a small bowl, add the oil and lemon juice and stir to combine.

2   Leave to sit for at least 1 hour to infuse the flavours. This should keep in an airtight container in the fridge for up 3 weeks.

SALSA VERDE

We use this popular sauce liberally and so should you, as it is so versatile and works well with so many things. This is our version, but don't feel limited by the recipe. If you are missing an ingredient, try substituting it or leave it out all together. The important thing to remember is that you should not use hard herbs such as rosemary or thyme as they will give the sauce an unpleasant texture. Adding coriander, chilli or even green tomatoes will give you a spicier version, while tarragon and vinegar are more classic additions. You can also play around with the fineness and coarseness of the sauce, depending on how you prefer it. Sometimes, we like to finely chop our herbs and other times almost tear them. Enjoy it on salads, vegetables and pretty much all meats too.

MAKES ABOUT 1 CUP
Handful of basil leaves, finely chopped
Handful of flat-leaf parsley leaves, finely chopped
Small handful of mint leaves, finely chopped
1 tbsp capers, chopped
3 anchovies, chopped
1 garlic clove, very finely chopped
Zest and juice of 1 unwaxed lemon
1 tsp Dijon mustard
60ml olive oil
Fine sea salt, to taste

1   Place the herbs, capers, anchovies, garlic, lemon zest and juice and mustard in a medium bowl. Pour in the olive oil and stir to combine, then season to taste with salt.

2   This will keep in an airtight container in the fridge for up to 3 days.

GOCHUJANG KETCHUP

On its own, gochujang tastes amazing and makes a great marinade, for lamb and pork in particular. The addition of the other ingredients brings sweetness and acidity that lift it to new heights. It is also killer on our Kimchi Pancake and Pork Belly brunch dish (see page 84). You should have little trouble finding gochujang (Korean fermented bean paste with chilli) these days; any Asian supermarket will stock it.

MAKES ABOUT 1½ CUPS
120g gochujang
60ml rice wine vinegar
160g tahini
80ml sesame oil
50ml soy sauce
80g caster sugar
50g Confit Garlic (see page 276), mashed with a fork

1   Place all the ingredients in a bowl and whisk together to combine. Let stand for 10 minutes to make sure the sugars have dissolved and the garlic has imparted its flavour.

2   This will keep in a airtight container in the fridge for up to 3 weeks.

STICKY SOY

This sticky reduction is a handy thing to have in the kitchen. It acts as dip for the Blue Cheese and Peanut Wontons (page 150) and works as a dressing for rare roast beef and smoked eel. It also works really well with a little garlic as the base reduction for a soy butter sauce.

MAKES ABOUT 1 CUP
250ml soy sauce
60g caster sugar
90ml kecap manis (sweet soy sauce)
Small thumb-sized piece of fresh ginger, peeled and sliced
60ml balsamic vinegar

1   Put all the ingredients into a pan and place over a high heat. Bring to the boil then reduce the heat and simmer gently for about 30 minutes until the liquid has reduced by half.

2   Set aside to cool then place in an airtight container and store in the fridge; this will keep for up to 2 months. To use, bring back to room temperature or heat very gently – this will make it an easier consistency to use.

MOJO VERDE

Usually served as a raw condiment with potatoes, this sauce originates from the Canary Islands but its reach is far greater. I encountered a cooked version on a coffee-buying trip in Brazil, where it was served with fried cassava. There the translation seems to mean any sauce with garlic. When you cook the sauce out, the flavours soften and the result is a rounder, more deeply flavoured sauce. It is great with seafood and fish, and a red version, where you use red chilli instead of green and red onions and red pepper, goes brilliantly with meaty dishes. (MK)

MAKES ABOUT 1½ CUPS
50g mint leaves
60g coriander, leaves and stalks roughly chopped
60g flat-leaf parsley, leaves and stalks roughly chopped
1 green chilli, roughly chopped
1 brown onion, roughly chopped
5 garlic cloves, lightly crushed
300ml olive oil
1 tbsp red wine vinegar
1 tbsp fine sea salt
Juice of 1 lemon

1   Place the mint, coriander, parsley, chilli, onion, garlic and olive oil in a food processor and blitz to a paste.

2   Transfer the paste to a small pan with a tight-fitting lid and gently heat, covered, over a medium heat until it starts to bubble. Turn the heat down and continue to cook for a further 25 minutes until the colour has dulled and the oil has separated.

3   Remove from the heat and transfer to a small bowl or container. Add the vinegar, salt and lemon juice.

4   Use as you need it – this will keep in the fridge in an airtight container for up to 2 weeks.

SICHUAN CHILLI OIL

I first made this as a condiment to be served with the Chicken and Rice on page 222. I got fed up of running out of chilli oil and having to go and buy it from a Chinese supermarket. Now we serve it with Smashed Cucumbers too (see page 122). It gets better and better with time so make a full recipe and keep it in your fridge to mature. (MK)

MAKES ABOUT 2 CUPS
2 thumb-sized pieces of fresh ginger, peeled
1 tbsp cumin seeds, toasted and ground
2 tbsp chilli powder
4 tbsp Sichuan peppercorns
5 tbsp gochugaru, or other red pepper flakes
2 tbsp Chinese five spice
2 tbsp sesame seeds, toasted
2 garlic cloves, very finely chopped
400ml vegetable oil
3 star anise
2 bay leaves

1   Thinly slice one of the pieces of ginger and set aside. Finely chop the other piece and put in a heavy bowl with the cumin seeds, chilli powder, Sichuan peppercorns, 2 tablespoons of the gochugaru, the Chinese five spice, sesame seeds and garlic. Place a sieve over the bowl and set aside.

2   In a pan, combine the vegetable oil, sliced ginger, star anise, bay leaves and remaining gochugaru. Gently heat the oil and aromats over a low heat until the mixture is bubbling and the ginger is beginning to brown around the edges.

3   While the oil is still hot, pour it into the sieve over the spice mixture in the bowl. Discard the aromats in the sieve and set the bowl of spiced oil aside to cool.

4   Once cool, store in an airtight container in the fridge for up to 1 month. It will improve with time.

SOUR PICKLED RED ONIONS

As with most instant pickles, fresh is best. They will
still taste good for a few hours, but over time they
will lose the crunchy texture that makes them great.
Slice the onions as thickly or as thinly as you like,
depending on what you are using them for.

MAKES ABOUT 1 CUP
150g red onions, sliced
5g salt
50ml red wine vinegar
50ml balsamic vinegar
30g muscovado sugar

1   Put the sliced onions in a medium bowl.
    In a separate bowl, combine the salt, vinegars
    and sugar, stirring to dissolve the sugar.

2   Pour the vinegar and sugar mixture over the
    onions and mix well with a spoon. Leave to stand
    for 10 minutes and then serve.

KIMCHI

Love it or hate it, kimchi is now in the general public's
culinary vernacular. If you are a fan, try this recipe.
It tastes way better than shop-bought and you can be
sure it doesn't have any nasty additives.

MAKES A 2 LITRE KILNER JAR
1 Chinese cabbage (about 1kg)
2 tbsp fine sea salt
5 tbsp gochugaru (red pepper flakes)
5 tbsp nam pla (fish sauce)
5 tbsp rice wine vinegar
2 garlic cloves, chopped
Thumb-sized piece of fresh ginger, peeled and chopped
½ large onion, chopped
Bunch of coriander stalks
1 tbsp caster sugar (or grated palm sugar)

1   Sterilise a 2-litre Kilner jar by scrubbing well
    and then rinsing with boiling water. (Alternatively
    you can use it straight from the dishwasher.)

2   Slice the cabbage in half through the core
    lengthways. Then cut each piece into three, again
    lengthways through the core. Next, remove the
    core, then cut your six long pieces in half
    horizontally. Put the cabbage into a large bowl,
    add the salt and massage through the cabbage.
    Set aside for 20 minutes.

3   Meanwhile put all the remaining ingredients
    into a food processor and blend together to form
    a paste.

4   You now need to rinse the salt from the cabbage.
    Cover the cabbage with cold water, allow to soak
    for 2 minutes then drain thoroughly. Repeat this
    soaking and draining step twice more. After
    the final rinse, make sure you drain the cabbage
    well on a clean tea towel.

5   Pour the pepper paste mixture over the cabbage
    and mix with your hands so that all of the
    cabbage is covered with paste. Place each piece of
    cabbage into the sterilised jar and then pour in
    any excess paste. Pack the cabbage in tightly
    then leave on your work surface, uncovered, for
    24 hours until fermentation begins. Then seal
    the lid and place in the fridge for at least a week
    before you intend to use it.

PRESERVED LEMONS

The process to create the final product may take
a while from start to finish but the results are entirely
worth it. These will taste significantly better than
any preserved lemon you can find in the shops.
We highly recommend having a jar of these in your
fridge at all times. They are so versatile and can be
used to lift any dish that requires a salty, citrus punch.

MAKES A 2 LITRE KILNER JAR
400g fine sea salt
1 tbsp cumin seeds, toasted
1 tbsp coriander seeds, toasted
1 tbsp black peppercorns
6 thyme sprigs
4 bay leaves
8 unwaxed lemons
Juice of 6 lemons (or enough to cover the lemons)

1   Sterilise a 2-litre jar with a sealable lid by
    scrubbing well and then rinsing with boiling
    water. (Alternatively you can use it straight
    from the dishwasher.)

2   In a large bowl combine the salt, cumin seeds,
    coriander seeds, peppercorns, thyme and
    bay leaves.

3   Wash the lemons and then cut a cross into each
    one, nearly to the base but so that the quarters
    stay together. Push the salt mixture into the
    middle of the lemons, completely filling them.

4   Push the lemons into the sterilised jar, packing
    them down firmly and pouring in the remaining
    salt mixture in stages. Pour over the lemon juice,
    making sure the lemons are completely covered.
    Close the lid and leave at room temperature in
    a cool, dark place for 1–2 days, then transfer to
    the fridge.

5   Over the next 4 weeks regularly check to ensure
    the lemons are completely covered in liquid. We
    usually give them a good turn over and a squash
    to make sure they stay covered before placing
    back in the fridge. After 4 weeks, the lemons
    should be ready to use and they will last in the
    fridge for up to 12 months.

SHICHIMI TOGARASHI

Shichimi togarashi is a Japanese spice mix containing
seven ingredients, generally always with chilli. This
is our version and it is a great seasoning agent that
can elevate the flavour of a salad, a bowl of noodles or
a ceviche to new heights. It brings a subtle, balanced
and refreshing spice to the party.

MAKES ABOUT 1 CUP
4 tbsp sancho pepper, toasted (or use black peppercorns
if unavailable)
3 tbsp Japanese red chilli flakes
½ nori sheet, toasted
2 tbsp dried orange peel
10 slices of garlic, fried until crisp
2 tbsp sesame seeds
2 tbsp hemp seeds

1   Grind the sancho, chilli flakes, nori and orange
    peel to a medium-fine powder using a mortar
    and pestle.

2   Add the fried garlic and pound to combine and
    spread the garlic flavour. Finally add the hemp
    and sesame seeds.

3   Store in an airtight jar for up to 1 month.

SICHUAN SALT AND PEPPER SEASONING

This fantastic seasoning started life at Caravan on our first ever menu with fried baby squid. The balance of heat, citrus zing and salt is truly delicious. We have subsequently used it with many dishes including, sweetcorn and grilled quail (see pages 138 and 212).

MAKES ABOUT ½ CUP
1 tbsp Sichuan peppercorns
1 cinnamon stick
3 star anise
1 tsp coriander seeds
80 fine sea salt
30g caster sugar
Zest of 2 unwaxed lemons
Zest 4 limes

1   Preheat the oven to 200°C and place a heavy-based roasting dish in the oven while it heats up.

2   Toast the Sichuan peppercorns, cinnamon, star anise and coriander seeds in a heavy-based pan over a gentle heat. Once they begin to smell aromatic and begin to brown, you know they are ready. Use a mortar and pestle to pound the spices to a fine powder, then transfer to a small mixing bowl. Add the salt and sugar and stir to combine.

3   Remove the roasting dish from the oven, and grate the zest of the lemons and limes directly onto the base of the dish; allow it to stand for 5 minutes. Once the zest has dried out, combine it with the ingredients in the mixing bowl.

4   Store in an airtight container in a cool, dry place for up to 1 week.

GARAM MASALA

You could buy this from a supermarket, but it will never be as good as if you make it from scratch. It keeps for a couple of weeks in a cool, dry place so it is worth the effort to make this fresh.

MAKES ABOUT ½ CUP
1 tsp black peppercorns
½ tsp cloves
5 cardamom pods
1 tbsp cumin seeds
1 tbsp coriander seeds
1 cinnamon stick
4 tbsp dried red chilli flakes
½ nutmeg, grated

1   Place the peppercorns, cloves, cardamom, cumin seeds, coriander seeds and cinnamon in a large frying pan over a medium heat and toast, shaking the pan regularly, until the spices smell aromatic – around 3–4 minutes.

2   Remove the spices from the pan and grind to a powder using a mortar and pestle or a spice grinder. Add the chilli flakes and nutmeg and stir through. This will keep in an airtight container in a cool, dark place for up to 2 weeks.

MASTER STOCK

This is the most delicious and versatile braising liquor that just keeps on giving – it gets better and better the more you use it, in a similar fashion to a mother for sourdough baking. Each time you use it, the stock imparts its flavour into the protein you are cooking and in the same way the protein you are cooking adds a depth of flavour to the stock. Every time you use the stock, use a fresh round of aromatics, bring it to the boil and pour it over whatever you are braising.

MAKES JUST OVER 1 LITRE
1.2 litres water
200ml soy sauce
1 red chilli
Thumb-sized piece (50g) of fresh ginger
1 whole garlic bulb, sliced in half horizontally
2 spring onions
4 star anise
15g dried tangerine peel (or use a piece of fresh orange peel)
1 cinnamon stick
10 coriander stalks
50g palm sugar

1   Place all ingredients into a medium pan and bring to the boil. Reduce the heat and simmer for 30 minutes, then allow to cool. Store in an airtight container in the fridge.

CHICKEN STOCK

If you are making chicken stock from scratch then use this recipe. The basic idea is always the same but do not be afraid to throw in other ingredients if you wish. Don't be precious and load your stock with flavour. Just avoid adding vegetables that will break down as they cook – potatoes and cabbage, for example, will make your stock cloudy.

MAKES 3 LITRES
4 raw chicken carcasses (ask your butcher)
2 medium brown onions, roughly chopped
3 garlic cloves
4–5 celery sticks, roughly chopped
1 small leek, roughly chopped
1 carrot
8 black peppercorns
4 bay leaves
6 thyme sprigs
5 litres water

1   Place the chicken carcasses into a large stockpot, add all the vegetables and herbs and pour over the water to completely cover the bones.

2   Place over a high heat and bring to a rolling boil, removing any scum that rises to the surface. Reduce the heat and simmer slowly for 4 hours. Keep checking the stock throughout this, skimming off any residue that has risen to the surface.

3   Carefully remove the carcasses and then strain the liquid through a sieve. Allow to cool before storing in the fridge for up to 3 days. Alternatively, you can freeze in smaller amounts for up to 3 months.

FRIED SHALLOTS

Fried shallots have been a go-to garnish for us for as long as we can remember. They have added a sweetness and a crunch to so many soup, salad and vegetable dishes over the years that we almost got sick of them. Almost. They are best used on the day they are made.

MAKES ABOUT 1 CUP
250g shallots, thinly sliced into rings
150ml vegetable oil

1   Rinse the sliced shallots in cold water in a small bowl, then drain thoroughly ad pat dry with kitchen paper.

2   Heat the oil in a large frying pan, add the shallots and fry over a low heat for 10–15 minutes until brown but still soft. Remove from the pan and allow to cool on kitchen paper.

TARO CRISPS

Taro is a root vegetable used extensively in Asian and Pacific Island cuisines. Similar to potatoes, they are a great dish filler when boiled but they come to life and are at their best when thinly sliced and fried. They add an excellent crunch and a beautiful look to a salad or ceviche, thanks to the characteristic purple veins that run from the centre of the taro to the outer rim.

200g taro
800ml vegetable oil, for deep-frying
Fine sea salt, to taste

1   Line a large flat tray with a double layer of absorbent kitchen paper.

2   Peel the taro then slice them as thinly as you can – use a mandolin if you have one as it's important that slices are a uniform thickness so that they cook at a uniform rate.

3   Heat the oil in a high-sided pan to a temperature 170°C. Test this by dropping in a single taro slice; if it sizzles immediately it is ready.

4   Working in batches so you don't overcrowd the pan, drop the sliced taro into the oil. Cook each batch for approximately 3 minutes or until golden brown and crisp. Once the taro is crisp, carefully lift the crisps from the oil and place them on the kitchen paper to drain. Sprinkle with sea salt while they are still warm.

5   Allow to cool then use within 2 days.

ABOUT THE AUTHORS

Chris Ammermann is the founder and operations director of Caravan. He loves people, hospitality and a good system.

Laura Harper-Hinton is the founder and creative director of Caravan. She loves beautiful food and design, grey, and her tape measure.

Miles Kirby is the founder and chef director of Caravan. He loves all things food and drink, beautiful spaces and efficient storage solutions.

Caravan started with a friendship and a passion for food, creativity and hospitality. The three founders met while working in a bustling restaurant and bar in Wellington, new Zealand over 20 years ago. Chris served the drinks, Miles made the food and Laura welcomed the guests. Over many a late night and too much tequila, the idea that would become Caravan was born. Extensive travelling followed before the team landed in the UK and immersed themselves in London hospitality. Much eating, drinking and long working hours followed and the idea of combining house-roasted coffee and 'well-travelled' food, available all day in a relaxed informal setting, eventually crystallised.
The rest, as they say, is history.

THANKS GO TO

Rowan Yapp and the team at Square Peg; Issy Croker (photographer); David Lane (design); Hannah Meri Williams (design); Clare Sayer (copy-editor); Shamina Somani and Renée Williams (stylists); Charlie Brotherstone (our agent).

Tanya and the PR team at Gerber; Toby Kidman, our operations director; Matt Burgess, our group head chef; all beautiful Caravan staff past and present.

All our amazing friends and family who have supported us along the way, with whom we have shared many a drink and a meal and without whom we would have no reprieve.

The people who have inspired us and for whom we have great respect: Peter Gordon, Anna Hansen, Jonathan Rutherfurd Best, Margot and Fergus Henderson, Nick Lander, Roger Madelin, Andrew Higgie, Al Brown, Ratnesh Bagdai to name but a few.

1 3 5 7 9 10 8 6 4 2

Square Peg, an imprint of Vintage,
20 Vauxhall Bridge Road,
London SW1V 2SA

Square Peg is part of the Penguin
Random House group of companies
whose addresses can be found at
global.penguinrandomhouse.com.

Penguin
Random House
UK

First published by Square Peg in 2017

Penguin.co.uk/vintage

A CIP catalogue record for this book
is available from the British Library

ISBN 9781910931233

Design by Lane & Associates
Photography by Issy Croker
Prop styling by Shamina Somani
and Renée Williams

Food styling by Miles Kirby, Matt
Burgess and Laura Harper-Hinton

Printed and bound in China by
C&C Offset Printing Co. Ltd

Penguin Random House is committed
to a sustainable future for our business,
our readers and our planet. This
book is made from Forest Stewardship
Council® certified paper.